MW00777191

I & II Thessalonians

PREPARING FOR THE SECOND COMING

MIKE MAZZALONGO

BibleTalk.TV

Line by Line Bible Studies

Line by line, verse by verse. These studies are designed to bring out the simple meaning of the biblical text for the modern reader.

ISBN: 978-0-69242-040-9

BibleTalk Books
14998 E. Reno
Choctaw, Oklahoma 73020

TABLE OF CONTENTS

1.
INTRODUCTION TO I THESSALONIANS

> Therefore be on the alert, for you do not know which day your Lord is coming. But be sure of this, that if the head of the house had known at what time of the night the thief was coming, he would have been on the alert and would not have allowed his house to be broken into. For this reason you also must be ready; for the Son of Man is coming at an hour when you do not think He will.
> - Matthew 24:42-44

When I was a child my parents taught me to be prepared for the next day: school clothes ready, homework done, no going out on weeknights. I am grateful to them because their early lessons molded my work habits of today and helped me succeed in my career. When I became a disciple of Jesus I learned that this principle of preparedness was true in Christian living as well.

As Christians we must also prepare, but not just for tomorrow – we must prepare for that day when Jesus will return because when that day comes, there will be no tomorrow! Paul's epistles to the Thessalonians were written with the purpose of encouraging these Christians to be ready for the last day when Jesus would return, a day that could have happened in their lifetimes but didn't. This means that the last day could happen during our lifetimes, so we will study these letters in order to prepare should that day come to us.

Background

Since this will be a formal study of this first epistle, I'd like to begin by giving you some introductory information about the place and circumstances in which this congregation was established.

Thessalonica - The City

The Thessalonica mentioned in Paul's letters is the modern day city of Salonika in South Eastern Europe. It is between Romania and Bulgaria to the north, Yugoslavia and Albania to the west. It is (as it was in the first century) a port city in central Macedonia, Greece on the edge of the Aegean Sea. Today it has a population of about 500,000 people.

The city was originally built in 315 BC by the Macedonian king, Cassander, and named after his wife who was Alexander the Great's half-sister. Because of its location, Thessalonica became a natural seaport and was a main route from Rome to the east. It was the largest trading center for the region of Macedonia with a population of 200,000 at that time. Thessalonica was within sight of Mount Olympus – a real mountain range that was believed to be the home of the gods in Greek mythology. Because of its location Thessalonica became a wealthy, cosmopolitan city where many cultures converged (Roman, Greek). Because it was a commercial center there was also a colony of Jews who lived and traded there and who had built a synagogue in order to practice their ancient religion in the midst of this worldly, pagan and wicked place. It was into this city in the year 51 AD that Paul found his way after receiving a vision or calling from the Lord.

Thessalonica - The Church

The church in Thessalonica was established there in approximately 51 AD while Paul was on his second missionary journey. The book of Acts recounts the events surrounding the founding of this congregation.

The Vision

Paul, Silas and Timothy were traveling on their second journey and in the process of strengthening churches established on the first journey when they had a "vision" or "calling."

> They passed through the Phrygian and Galatian region, having been forbidden by the Holy Spirit to speak the word in Asia; and after they came to Mysia, they were trying to go into Bithynia, and the Spirit of Jesus did not permit them; and passing by Mysia, they came down to Troas. A vision appeared to Paul in the night; a man of Macedonia was standing and appealing to him, and saying, "Come over to Macedonia and help us." When he had seen the vision, immediately we sought to go into Macedonia, concluding that God had called us to preach the gospel to them.
> - Acts 16:6-10

Philippi

They crossed the Aegean Sea and made their way to Philippi, where through a series of events they established a church there.

> So putting out to sea from Troas, we ran a straight course to Samothrace, and on the day following to Neapolis; and from there to Phillipi, which is a leading city of the district of Macedonia, a Roman colony; and we were staying in this city for some days. And on the Sabbath day we went outside the gate to a riverside, where we were supposing that there would be a place of prayer; and we sat down and began speaking to the women who had assembled. A woman named Lydia,

> from the city of Thyatira, a seller of purple fabrics, a worshiper of God, was listening, and the Lord opened her heart to respond to the things spoken by Paul. And when she and her household had been baptized, she urged us, saying, "If you have judged me to be faithful to the Lord, come into my house and stay." And she prevailed upon us.
> - Acts 16:11-15

Later on we read that their presence and activities stir up a riot and they are jailed but miraculously released. After gaining their freedom they make their way a hundred miles south and come to the city of Thessalonica.

Thessalonica

Luke recounts the church being planted there and describes the further troubles encountered by the missionaries.

> Now when they had traveled through Amphiplis and Apollonia, they came to Thessalonica, where there was a synagogue of the Jews. And according to Paul's custom, he went to them, and for three Sabbaths reasoned with them from the Scriptures, explaining and giving evidence that the Christ had to suffer and rise again from the dead, and saying, "This Jesus whom I am proclaiming to you is the Christ." And some of them were persuaded and joined Paul and Silas, along with a large number of the God-fearing Greeks and a number of the leading women. But the Jews, becoming jealous and taking along some wicked men from the market place, formed a mob and set the city in an uproar, and attacking the house of Jason, they were seeking to bring them out to the people. When they did not find them, they began dragging Jason and some brethren before the city authorities, shouting, "These men who have upset the world have come here also; and Jason has welcomed them, and they all

> act contrary to the decrees of Caesar, saying that there is another king, Jesus. They stirred up the crowd and the city authorities heard these things. And when they had received a pledge from Jason and the others, they released them. The brethren immediately sent Paul and Silas away by night to Berea, and when they arrived, they went into the synagogue of the Jews.
> - Acts 17:1-10

So we see that Paul spent about a month here before being chased to the neighboring city of Berea some 50 miles west. This was not a lot of teaching time for a newly established church.

Corinth

Paul spent some time in Berea teaching before moving on to Athens in southern Greece, leaving Timothy and Silas in Berea. Paul made a few converts in Athens and his sermon on Mars Hill to the Athenian philosophers is recorded in Acts 17. He soon left Athens and headed for his final destination in Greece which was the city of Corinth. It is during his 18 months in Corinth that Paul wrote the two letters sent to the Thessalonians.

Occasion and Date of I Thessalonians

Once Timothy arrived in Corinth to be with Paul he began to report on the progress of the young churches that they had established in the region. When it came to Thessalonica, Timothy brought news that these young Christians were bearing well the persecution they were under because of their faith. He did mention, however, that several of their number had died and they were confused as to what would happen to those who died before the Lord returned. Paul had taught them that Jesus was to return but they hadn't considered the idea that some of them might die before this event actually took place. And so Paul, not very long after he had established this church, writes to them in order to calm their fears and provide further instructions concerning the second coming of the Lord.

This Thessalonian letter is the earliest full discussion related to the second coming of Christ and the resurrection of the saints (written before Revelation). Scholars have no doubts concerning the authorship of this letter since Paul names himself, and historians note that it was widely distributed and accepted by the early church – two key factors in determining the authenticity and inspiration of New Testament documents. It is a model epistle when examining the various growing pains experienced by a new church. The Thessalonian congregation had been established and taught in the span of a few weeks. They were now facing persecution as well as confusion about doctrine. And so Paul writes to them in order to calm their fears and teach them what they wanted to understand but couldn't because of their lack of information and teaching.

Main Outline - I Thessalonians

This letter deals with three main themes that make up the body of the letter and these are book-ended by a salutation at the beginning and an exhortation and final greeting at the end. A basic outline would look like this:

1. Paul's Prayer of Thanksgiving – 1:1-10

2. Paul Defends His Conduct Among Them – 2:1-3:13

3. Paul Exhorts the Thessalonians to Purer Conduct – 4:1-12

4. Paul Reveals Jesus' Teaching Concerning the End – 4:13-5:3

5. Paul Instructs the Church in Preparing for the End – 5:4-28

General Purposes of the Letter

As we go through the first letter we will see some things that Paul is trying to accomplish with this brief epistle.

To Express His Feelings

In the opening section we will see Paul expressing his joy and gratitude for their fidelity and loyalty to Paul and his helpers. They were a young church and Paul hadn't been with them long, however they were faithful in many ways despite the attacks leveled against them and their faith. A great reward for ministers is seeing the faithfulness and growth of the members. Nothing kills the zeal of the preacher or missionary more than unfaithful Christians. This is why many leave to go to other places seeking new fields to harvest and more fruitful members.

Paul Defends Himself

After his departure there were some who accused Paul of being insincere, of being a fraud. He spends time in this letter defending his conduct. The best way to cause division is to attack the leaders and teachers in the church. This tactic was being used by certain people in the Thessalonian church against the Apostle.

Paul Encourages Them

Their new faith was being tested and many were being tempted to return to their pagan lifestyles with its sexual impurity. Not many begin the Christian life and even fewer finish because they don't expect to be tested, and when they are – they quit. Paul encourages them to remain faithful to Christ despite the trials and temptations.

Paul Gives Them Further Teaching

He provides teaching in two critical areas:

1. The details concerning the second coming of Christ. This idea is mentioned 20 times in the two letters.

2. Sanctified living. The second coming was the reason for the purified living of Christians. Paul explained this in more detail.

Fellowship

Paul encourages them and sends greetings to maintain love and fellowship between his group and these young Christians.

Summary

This is some of the background information needed to help you understand the material we will look at as we begin this series. In the meantime, some closing remarks concerning the relevance of this study for us today.

We study this epistle because, in many ways, it is a portrait of ourselves. We are a small group surrounded by a large, secular and immoral society. It is always a temptation to return to a worldly lifestyle.

We study this to gain a better understanding about the end of the world and the various teachings about these matters. We should know what the Bible teaches about the Man of Lawlessness, the rapture, tribulation and what happens at the end of time. We need to get a handle on these things and try to separate fact from fantasy.

Finally, we study to better prepare ourselves for the return of the Lord. He may come sooner than later, but we need to be ready in any case. These two letters to the Thessalonians will help us in this effort.

2.
GENUINE CONVERSION

Let's review the main points of study before moving on to the text of I Thessalonians.

1. Thessalonica was an important port city in Macedonia – cosmopolitan, rich, worldly.

2. Paul established a church here in 51 AD when he spent approximately a month preaching in the local synagogue.

3. He was run out of town by Jewish leaders and eventually made his way to Corinth, which was in southern Greece.

4. After receiving a report from Timothy concerning the progress and problems the Thessalonians were having since his departure, he writes two letters to this young church in order to:

    - Express his joy of their faithfulness
    - Defend his conduct while among them
    - Encourage them
    - Give them more teaching on specific matters

We are studying these epistles so that, like the Thessalonians, we too can understand more about the second coming, and be prepared for it.

Salutation – I Thessalonians 1:1

The first section of this epistle is the salutation and it is contained in the first verse.

> Paul and Silvanus and Timothy, to the church of the Thessalonians in God the Father and the Lord Jesus Christ: Grace to you and peace.
> - I Thessalonians 1:1

Note that as an apostle Paul puts his name first; Silvanus (which was the Roman name of Silas) is mentioned second because he was chosen to accompany Paul on the second missionary journey once Barnabas and Mark went their own way to Cyprus; Timothy is last because he is the youngest.

He refers to them as the church or the "called out" among the Thessalonians. They were called to come out from the Thessalonian city to be with God through Christ. This is what the term "church" means.

Grace and peace are the normal ways Paul uses to greet brethren. Grace is what you receive, all the spiritual blessings in Christ. Peace is what these blessings (forgiveness, adoption, righteousness, etc.) make you feel. Peace is the end result of grace.

Note how Paul puts all the names on an equal footing:

- God – Supreme Being
- Father – same as
- Lord – Greek word for Jehovah
- Jesus – Lord's human name (Joshua)
- Christ – Lord's title

The word "father" means source and is not a reference to "maleness" but to origin.

Paul begins by putting God and Jesus as equal, and himself, his co-workers and his readers as one single unit within the circle of the Godhead.

Thanksgiving – 1:2-10

In the next section Paul goes from his salutation of these people to the giving of thanks to God because of them.

> We give thanks to God always for all of you, making mention of you in our prayers.
> - I Thessalonians 1:2

When Paul and the others pray, they give thanks because when they remember the Thessalonians they recall the things that God has done in their lives.

> Constantly bearing in mind your work of faith and labor of love and steadfastness of hope in our Lord Jesus Christ in the presence of our God and Father, knowing, brethren beloved by God, His choice of you;
> - I Thessalonians 1:3-4

Paul describes 4 things that they remember about these people that cause them to give thanks.

1. Their work of faith – this refers to the things they did because of their faith. It also confirms that they had the right kind of faith: faith that worked and served. Faith that doesn't work is not true faith.

2. Labor of love – this signifies and emphasizes the intensity of their work: it was hard work, it was an effort, it caused fatigue as true work often does. It was a labor of love in that those who worked because of faith persevered even when tired, because of their love. The effort, inconvenience, and expense of serving the church is not given because it's a pleasure – it is given because you love and you love because you believe.

3. The steadiness of their hope – there is a difference between "wishing" and the idea of Biblical hope. For example, the lazy student only wishes he will pass the final exam; the good student has hope/confidence that he will pass.

The Thessalonians had biblical hope (confident expectation – not just cross my fingers and make a wish kind of hope). They were confident that God would deliver on His promise of eternal life. Their perseverance in loving service was sparked by their initial faith and kept alive by their unswerving hope/confidence in God and His promises.

When you lose hope it is usually a sign that your faith and love are weak. Paul says that all of these things are done in the presence of God who accepts our love but sees past our loving work to the faith that motivates it (man only sees the work, God sees the faith) and because of this He guarantees and strengthens our hope of eternal life. This creates a life affirming cycle that produces peace and joy in our hearts.

4. Genuine conversion – in seeing their faith, hope and love Paul is reassured that they are truly chosen of God and loved by God. We know we are sons of God because of this working faith, sustaining love and enduring hope. This is how we can know the true from the fake. Paul is also assured of their position with God because of the circumstances surrounding the time when they became Christians. He knew and was assuring them that theirs was a genuine conversion for four reasons he mentions in the following verses:

The message they heard was from God.

> For our gospel did not come to you in word only, but also in power and in the Holy Spirit and with full conviction;
> - I Thessalonians 1:5a

Paul and his workers were motivated by the power/inspiration of the Holy Spirit since it was a vision that initially brought them to Macedonia. They knew that it was God's word that they spoke and not man's (like the false teachers that were harassing many churches of that time). The messengers were fully convicted concerning their message – that it was truly from God they had no doubt. This should be the same criteria for our own salvation.

- Has what we believed come from God or man-made religion?
- What gives us courage to reach out to others is not the size of our church but the power of the message.
- If it is God's message then we have all the power we will ever need.

They knew their conversion was genuine because:

The messengers were godly.

> just as you know what kind of men we proved to be among you for your sake.
> - I Thessalonians 1:5b

Not only was the message from God, the messengers acted in a godly way. The power of the message is regulated by the quality of the messenger. (i.e. Which would be more valuable to you: a printed invitation addressed to you to attend a special occasion or email in your spam folder?)

The Apostles had a clear conscience and acted honorably among the new converts because their message was credible. Sometimes we're not effective in winning others to Christ because our example is interfering with the message. If a person doesn't see anything special in you because of Christ, why should they believe? Paul knew that his conduct was perfectly in line with the message he preached.

They knew their conversion was genuine because:

The message produced a change.

> You also became imitators of us and of the Lord, having received the word in much tribulation with the joy of the Holy Spirit,
> - I Thessalonians 1:6

The Thessalonians began imitating the Apostles as the Apostles imitated the Lord. How? They were convinced that the message was from God Himself, just as the Apostles were convinced when they received it from Jesus. They improved their conduct and they obeyed the word despite the pressure from the Jews and pagans around them. They maintained a joyful heart despite hardship and persecution, just like the Apostles did.

The truest proof of a sincere conversion to Jesus Christ is a change in lifestyle. The greater the change, the greater the assurance of a full and complete conversion. If you're not any different now than you were before you became a Christian, you're not really born again, you've merely changed religions. Lots of people change their religion for a variety of reasons, only converted people change their hearts, like the Thessalonians.

Finally, Paul knew and was thankful for their true conversion because:

They became the message.

> So that you became an example to all the believers in Macedonia and in Achaia. For the word of the Lord has sounded forth from you, not only in Macedonia and Achaia, but also in every place your faith toward God has gone forth, so that we have no need to say anything. For they themselves report about us what kind of a reception we had with you, and how you turned to God from idols to serve a living and true God, and to wait for His son from heaven, whom He raised from the dead, that is Jesus, who rescues us from the wrath to come.
> - I Thessalonians 1:7-10

The Apostle had no need to speak about this church, the fact that they had responded with enthusiasm, obedience and perseverance was an inspiration to all other believers. As Christians we not only have a duty to the lost but also to other believers in other congregations to be a light of encouragement. You must become the voice of God to the lost and a voice of encouragement to the brethren in order to be fully mature.

Summary

Let's summarize this opening section. Paul is writing to this young church that he has established and he is rejoicing and giving thanks for them in his opening prayer. He is thankful because he is sure that they are God's chosen children for two main reasons:

1. He is sure of their conversion

He is sure that they received God's word from God's workers in a godly way. He sees that their conversion has produced the proper results: a changed lifestyle, hard work, faithfulness, hope for heaven and a loving heart. Many times people run into spiritual trouble because they are not careful about examining their conversion. When people are not taught correctly at conversion, they don't persevere for very long. It is proper to examine carefully how a person came to Christ to make sure that it was done in accordance to God's word, and not man's religious ideas.

2. Paul rejoices because of their growth

Paul is happy because he did his work properly and God is blessing it with a rich harvest of faith, hope and love among the Thessalonians. This should motivate us to do our work carefully and strictly according to the Scriptures when studying with others. Aside from the relationship between Paul and this church that we see in these opening verses, there is also a very practical layout of the normal steps of development an individual should go through as he/she matures in Christ:

Step #1 - Conversion to imitation. Initial conversion develops into an effort to imitate our mentors and teachers in Christ. They are the models we try to emulate as we begin to turn away from our old life to our new one.

Step #2 - Imitation to example. The constant effort to imitate begins to bear fruit as we slowly change to resemble more mature and Christ-like Christians. Christians look alike, act in unison, go in the same direction.

Step #3 - Example to conversion. Our example begins to draw new converts who try to imitate us. This completes the cycle in our growth from converted to converter. We should examine ourselves to see where we are in the process, personally and congregationally.

3.

TRUE MINISTERS

Let's review what we have covered so far in our study of I Thessalonians.

Paul is writing to the young church he has established in Thessalonica. In the opening of his letter he rejoices over the fact that he considers them to be true converts for several reasons. Because he was a true apostle preaching the pure gospel in love and sincerity, they were converted in the right way by people who knew the gospel. He rejoices in his prayer because their response to the gospel was sincere. Their belief was sincere. Their change was real. Their perseverance became an inspiration to others.

In the next two chapters Paul will review his time with them and defend his ministry among them. There is no mention of it directly but by the nature of Paul's response it seems that he had come under attack, being charged with the accusation of acting like a charlatan. At the time there were "wandering preachers and philosophers" who went from place to place teaching and spreading various ideas and philosophies in exchange for money and prestige. Some were saying that Paul was no more than one of these types. And so in the next section Paul will lay down the credentials that all should look for in one who is a true minister of the word – whether he be an Apostle, evangelist or teacher.

Credentials for True Ministers - I Thessalonians 2:1-3:13

1. True Ministers Trust God - 2:1-2

> For you yourselves know, brethren, that our coming to you was not in vain, but after we had already suffered and been mistreated in Philippi, as you know, we had the boldness in our god to speak to you the gospel of God amid much opposition.
> - I Thessalonians 2:1-2

Paul's rescue from prison in Philippi; his coming to Macedonia; his trials and opposition by the Jews; all of these events were sustained and accomplished because he trusted in God. When you examine Paul's experiences you see that the only way he could have survived was through the Lord. He trusted God to rescue him from jail when the situation was hopeless. He trusted God for the opportunities to make contacts and preach because he was helpless to make these happen. He trusted God to give him direction for his ministry at a time that he was directionless. He trusted God to save him from his attackers when he was defenseless.

True leaders in ministry are not such simply because they are good speakers, debaters or organizers – they are just qualified to lead in ministry if they can demonstrate their abiding trust in God. Paul demonstrated this trust when he continued preaching and teaching despite the discouragement and opposition he faced in and out of the church. True leaders demonstrate this quality in the same way in today's church

2. True Ministers are Sincere – 2:3-12

Paul compares 2 sets of characteristics for judging ministers, preachers and leaders.

Worldly Characteristics – vs. 3-6

> For our exhortation does not come from error or impurity or by way of deceit; but just as we have been approved by God to be entrusted with the gospel, so we speak, not as pleasing men, but God who examines our hearts. For we never came with flattering speech, as you know, nor with a pretext for greed – God is witness – nor did we seek glory from men, either from you or from others, even though as apostles of Christ we might have asserted our authority.

"Error" – not an honest mistake or misunderstanding, but rather error that comes from an evil mind:

- Impurity – sexual impurity
- Deceit – planned lies, dishonesty
- Popularity – trying to gain approval by telling people what they want to hear
- Flattery – done in order to blind them, not build them up
- False pretenses – any type of covering to hide greed
- Personal glory – try to raise yourself above the others

Paul suggests that these are reasons some go into religious service, or what they hide under the cover of ministry.

Spiritual Characteristics – vs. 7-12

> But we proved to be gentle among you, as a nursing mother tenderly cares for her own children. Having so fond an affection for you, we were well-pleased to impart to you not only the gospel of God but also our own lives, because you had become very dear to us. For you recall, brethren, our labor and hardship, how working night and day so as not to be a burden to any of you, we proclaimed to you the gospel of God. You are witnesses, and so is God, how devoutly and uprightly and blamelessly we behaved toward you believers; just as you know how we were exhorting and encouraging and imploring each one of you as a father would his own children, so that you would walk in a manner worthy of the God who calls you into His own kingdom and glory.

- Gentle – example of a nursing mother.
- Self-sacrificing – they gave of themselves, not just doctrine. They risked their lives to teach them. Gave their hearts as well as the message.
- Hard-working – they worked night and day among them and took no money which was their right (II Corinthians 11:8-9). They worked for free because the Thessalonians were young and poor.
- Pure – their conduct was above reproach. No hint of evil.
- Fervent – they wanted the Thessalonians to please God and have eternal life with all their hearts and strength. This was their motive in ministry: the good of the church.

Paul reminds them about their experience with himself, Silas and Timothy and he challenges them to judge them not only on what they said and taught but also on their actions. Some say that it's not Christian to judge, but Paul says that the church can and should examine itself and its leaders to see if what they say is from God and if what they do is godly. There's a big difference between criticizing and complaining because things are not like we want them, and making a sober judgment on the accuracy and conduct of our leaders and ourselves.

True ministers of the gospel need to demonstrate good things in order to accomplish good things; if the inside is good it will show itself on the outside.

3. True Ministers Get Results – 2:13-16

> For this reason we also constantly thank God that when you received the word of God which you heard from us, you accepted it not as the word of men, but for what it really is, the word of God, which also performs its work in you who believe. For you, brethren, became imitators of the churches of God in Christ Jesus that are in Judea, for you also endured the same sufferings at the hands of your own countrymen, even as they did from the Jews, who both killed the Lord Jesus and the prophets and drove us out. They are not pleasing to God, but hostile to all men, hindering us from speaking to the Gentiles so that they may be saved; with the result that they always fill up the measure of their sins. But wrath has come upon them to the utmost.

We don't know how big the church was in Thessalonica and that is not always the best rule of measurement. We do know however that despite the opposition, difficult circumstances and short period of teaching there was a radical change among the Thessalonians. This change occurred because godly men preached God's message accurately and in a godly way. We know that growth doesn't always come right away, but if the other elements are in place – it does come! True ministers don't blame the church for lack of growth, they ask God to change them first so their impact can have a positive effect for growth. The church cannot grow beyond its leadership. Jesus said:

> It is enough for the disciple that he becomes as his teacher.
> Matthew 10:24

4. True Ministers Love the Church - 2:17-3:13

> But we, brethren, having been taken away from you for a short while – in person, not in spirit – were all the more eager with great desire to see your face. For we wanted to come to you – I, Paul, more than once – and yet Satan hindered us. For who is our hope or joy or crown of exultation? Is it not even you, in the presence of our Lord Jesus at His coming? For you are our glory and joy.
>
> Therefore when we could endure it no longer, we thought it best to be left behind at Athens alone, and we sent Timothy, our brother and God's fellow worker in the gospel of Christ, to strengthen and encourage you as to your faith, so that no one would be disturbed by these afflictions; for you yourselves know that we have been destined for this. For indeed when we were with you, we kept telling you in advance that we were going to suffer affliction; and so it came to pass, as you know. For this reason, when I could endure it no longer, I also sent to find out about your faith, for fear that the tempter might have tempted you, and our labor would be in vain.
>
> But now that Timothy has come to us from you, and has brought us good news of your faith and love, and that you always think kindly of us, longing to see us just as we also long to see you, for this reason, brethren, in all our distress and affliction we were comforted about you through your faith; for now

> we really live, if you stand firm in the Lord. For what thanks can we render to God for you in return for all the joy with which we rejoice before our God on your account, as we night and day keep praying most earnestly that we may see your face, and may complete what is lacking in your faith?
> Now may our God and Father Himself and Jesus our Lord direct our way to you; and may the Lord cause you to increase and abound in love for one another, and for all people, just as we also do for you; so that He may establish your hearts without blame in holiness before our God and Father at the coming of our Lord Jesus with all His saints.

Note Paul's attitude toward the brethren:

- He was eager to see them – vs. 17
- They are his glory and joy – vs. 20
- He needed to know of their conditions – vs. 5
- His emotional life was tied to theirs – vs. 8
- He prayed for them night and day – vs. 10
- He wanted only the best blessings for them – vs. 11-13

Paul loves these brethren because they are the precious fruit of his work in the Lord. It was his love of Christ that motivated him to go to them at first, but now it is his love of them that causes his joy and continued efforts among them. A young man who wanted to go into mission work asked me what he needed in order to succeed in this type of endeavor. Did he need language training, a trade or second income to fall back on, knowledge of different religions, a good support network? I told him that all these things were necessary and basic, but the most important thing he needed was love for the people he was trying to convert.

You see, it's the love for the church that will get you through the difficult moments when they disappoint you, speak against you, even sin and abandon the assembly. Only the sincere love of the souls you are reaching out to will keep you in ministry. Training and support will start you in ministry, but only an abiding love for souls will keep you ministering long after the excitement and newness have worn off.

Summary

In this section we have seen Paul defending his ministry among them against the charge that he was a religious fake or an opportunist of some kind. In his defense he describes the characteristics of those who are religious charlatans and alongside of these he lays down four main characteristics to look for in a true minister of God:

- True ministers love and trust God – completely.
- True ministers practice what they preach and it is evident.
- True ministers get results. And they do this because they bring the power of God to get results, which is the gospel (Romans 1:16).
- True ministers love the church. Their love is evident by what they sacrifice to serve it. There are many who at some point think they want to become ministers, teachers or elders. These need to ask themselves what God desires from His ministers: not just degrees, work methods, equipment, money. God wants trust, purity and devotion to the church that His Son died to create. It is these qualities of the heart that give light to the studies, direction to the methods of work and the results for our efforts at preaching and teaching.

4.
TRUE CHURCHES

Let's review what we've learned so far:

1. The Thessalonian letters were written by Paul to a young church that he had established in just a few weeks while on his second missionary journey through Macedonia.

2. This church had been faithful and growing despite the attacks on Paul by Jewish leaders and persecutions by the pagan society in which they lived.

3. As you recall, the first epistle begins with Paul:

    - Expressing his thanksgiving for the Thessalonian's faith and perseverance.

    - Next he defends his conduct among them by describing how true ministers are supposed to act and how this was the way he and his associates acted around them:

        - Trusting in God

        - Pure lifestyle

        - Hard working

        - Lovers of the church

4. In the last chapter I said that Paul shows us that true conversion begins with sincere ministers who preach the truth in love to people who receive the message as God's word and respond to it in faith and obedience.

Until this point Paul has discussed the nature of true conversion and true ministers. At this point we will look at some characteristics associated with the true church that belongs to Christ.

The Church Continually Purifies its Conduct - I Thessalonians 4:1-12

The key word here is continually. Many churches begin well but lack the desire to continue to purify and improve their conduct.

> Finally then, brethren, we request and exhort you in the Lord Jesus, that as you received from us instruction as to how you ought to walk and please God (just as you actually do walk), that you excel still more. For you know what commandments we gave you by the authority of the Lord Jesus.
> - I Thessalonians 4:1-2

Note that Paul tells the church that he knows that they are living in a way that pleases God; he now encourages them by the authority of Christ to continue to purify that lifestyle according to what he has, and will teach them. Question: Why give them this instruction? Answer: They live among great temptation and the only way to remain strong is to keep the commitment to continually strive to please God.

Some people grow tired of sermons and lessons encouraging the church to be careful and to work hard at improving. These are necessary however, because only a firm commitment to continued growth and purity will keep the church pure. Impure and uncommitted churches have no power to win souls to Christ and risk losing their own spiritual health. Paul did not want this to happen to the Thessalonians so he mentions three areas where they needed to purify their lives.

Sexual Purity – vs. 3-5

> For this is the will of God, your sanctification; that is, that you abstain from sexual immorality.
> - I Thessalonians 4:3

The word "sanctification" means to set something aside for a godly purpose. When we become Christians, our physical bodies are sanctified, are set aside for God's use. Bodies that belong to God are to be used for His glory. Sexual immorality (adultery, homosexuality, pornography, lewdness, evil desires) does not glorify God. If you extend this thought further you will see that God wants total sanctification for His church. Of course sanctification doesn't mean that we are to have no sex life; it means that even our sex life is under His control and for His glory.

When a husband and wife are expressing their love and desire within the intimacy and boundaries of marriage – God is glorified. Activities outside this blessed state dishonor God and the individuals.

> That each of you know how to possess his own vessel in sanctification and honor, not in lustful passion, like the Gentiles who do not know God.
> - I Thessalonians 4:4-5

Paul goes on to say that the way to achieve this is to continually struggle for the ownership of our bodies. Controlling our sexual impulses so they can be expressed in meaningful and acceptable ways – this honors God. Behaving like those who do not know God and allow their bodies to be used by every devilish passion they feel – this dishonors God. We can and should marry, but Paul says that there is a way to do it that is right and pleasing to God.

Sexuality was given by God to mankind, but God also gave laws to guide our natural sexuality in such a way that this powerful force will bless men and women, not destroy them. Rules of sexual conduct that honor and not dishonor God.

There also needs to be a purification in regards to:

Integrity in Business – vs. 6

> And that no man transgress and defraud his brother in the matter because the Lord is the avenger in all these things, just as we also told you before and solemnly warned you.
> - I Thessalonians 4:6

The pagan world of the first century was notable for two vices: sexual immorality and unchecked greed. Thessalonica was a large trading and business center so many of the members of the church were involved in trade. Without the type of laws and the checks and balances of our system today, unsavory and unscrupulous business practices were the norm at that time. Paul doesn't go into details or examples here, he simply warns them of the consequences of violating another person in these matters. ("Brother" in the sense of neighbor and not member of the church.)

Some individuals interpret this verse in another way, saying that Paul continues his warning about sexual sins warning that men in the church not commit adultery with each other's wives.

This is a true and biblical idea but doesn't fit well with what and how Paul is expressing himself here. The word "matter" is a commercial term which literally means a business matter or in matters of commerce. This was an evident problem in pagan society and Paul makes reference to it.

Apparently Paul has warned them of this before and repeats his warning that even these violations will not go unpunished.

> For God has not called us for the purpose of impurity, but in sanctification. So, he who rejects this is not rejecting man but the god who gives His Holy Spirit to you.
> - I Thessalonians 4:7-8

Paul summarizes the two first admonitions (a greater effort at purifying their sexual and business lives). He explains the reasons why they must continue to purify themselves in these areas:

1. They are new creatures

In Christian baptism we bury the old pagan, unclean, impure, greedy, dishonest person and we resurrect a completely new person – sanctified – or set apart for a new purpose.

This new life has a new focus, a new purpose, a new set of guidelines. This new life is about purity in thought and deed, a continual effort to strain out what is impure and ungodly.

We are saved because God loves us. We are sanctified because God has a purpose for our lives (which Paul will explain in the next section).

2. They will be judged

The "this" that Paul refers to is God Himself. The one who rejects (sets aside, annuls), puts aside not just a lifestyle, but also the very God who gives this lifestyle of sanctification; of on-going purification powered by and made possible by the Holy Spirit, who is given for this very purpose.

In Chapter 5:19 Paul will say, *"Do not quench the Spirit; do not despise prophetic utterances."* Here he cautions that to deny or ignore God's word has the effect of extinguishing or suffocating the power of the Spirit within Christians.

In this chapter Paul is saying the same thing except that the extinguishing of the Spirit and His effect on us is done by not pursuing purity and by rejecting the sanctified life God offers us in favor of our old life of sin. He doesn't spell it out but the end of the matter is plain. Woe to the one who rejects God and the Spirit empowered life He offers in order to pursue the old life of sexual impurity and worldly greed and dishonesty.

We know that these things can bring very real physical consequences:

- Sexual diseases
- Unwanted pregnancies / guilt / depression
- Enslavement to depraved habits
- Revenge from those we cheat and steal or take advantage of

Yes there are physical consequences, but Paul adds to these that there is also a spiritual consequence to these things and warns those who have been saved from the terrible spiritual consequences not to go back or they will be subject to judgment.

So let's remember what's going on in this chapter: Paul tells them that there are three things that they need to work on in order to continue purifying themselves: purify their sexual lives, purify their business dealings, and...

Purify Their Public Witness – vs. 9-12

Usually our sexual sins are done in secret, most people can't tell if we are sexually pure or not. Most folks assume we are and are shocked if they find out any different. Our greed is also something we try to cover up or justify in various ways. Christians can hide these kinds of sins from other people, but the ability to hide our sins from others does not give us power in affecting other people for Christ. It only fools others into thinking we're sincere when we're not.

What affects people for Christ, however, is a Christian living a purified life and doing it consciously and openly. If others don't see this, they will not be impacted by our message. This is the reason I don't use tobacco. Aside from the health and addiction hazards, I know that non-Christians are not very impressed with a Christian who is a moderate or social tobacco user – they expect better from us and so should we.

And so, in this final section we see Paul establishing new goals for them to strive for in addition to the faithfulness and perseverance that they've already demonstrated.

> Now as to the love of the brethren, you have no need for anyone to write to you, for you yourselves are taught by God to love one another; for indeed you do practice it toward all the brethren who are in Macedonia. But we urge you, brethren, to excel still more.
> - I Thessalonians 4:9-10

He has already taught them the basic lesson of Jesus, which is to love one another. They've already demonstrated faith, perseverance, hospitality and helped the brethren throughout the province so they are known as a loving church. Paul wants them to continue doing these things. Their witness within the church was excellent, but now the Apostle deals with what their witness of daily living should be in order to affect those outside the church.

> And to make it your ambition to lead a quiet life and attend to your own business and work with your hands, just as we commanded you.

> - I Thessalonians 4:11

Paul now gives them 3 things that are essential in order to lead a balanced life that provides a good witness to others outside the church:

Lead a quiet life

This doesn't mean that there is to be no excitement or no action. It refers to a quiet spirit, a calm heart as opposed to a worrisome attitude. Some people love drama and everything in their lives is a "big deal," they draw everyone else into their whirlwind. A quiet life is one where it is evident that God is in control.

Attend to your own business

A quiet heart usually minds its own business. I think we call this virtue discretion. Someone whose life is not always spilling over into everyone else's.

Work with your hands

This expression doesn't refer to manual labor exclusively. It means that your own hands/work supports you. If you're worried and minding everyone else's business, you don't have time to take care of your own. Christians should earn their own living, quietly mind their own affairs and live with security and peace of mind.

> So that you will behave properly toward outsides and not be in any need.
> - I Thessalonians 4:12

Here Paul explains why we should do these things.

1. Christians need to model a balanced, quiet, fruitful life as an alternative to the fretful existence of many non-believers.

2. Live this way so they don't become a burden on society. There's nothing worse than Christians who are supported by a non-Christian society because the Christian refuses to work.

Summary

Paul recognizes the progress of this young church and commends them for their growth. He encourages them to continually purify their lives by:

- Maintaining sexual purity
- Being upright and honest in their business affairs
- Establishing quiet, balanced and productive lives

In doing these things they will cooperate with the purifying work of the Holy Spirit in their lives, and they will avoid judgment. They will also provide an example of what the true church looks and acts like in providing a powerful witness for Christ to the world. Doing these things prepares us and the world for the second coming of Jesus, which is our ultimate task.

5.
PREPARING FOR THE END

The theme for our study has been, "Preparing for the Second coming" and our text has been the first epistle to the Thessalonians. In this letter Paul commends the Thessalonians for being a "true church." Today we often measure the authenticity of a church by:

- Size or influence
- The quality of the building
- The type of worship service
- The ministry staff (number and qualifications)

But Paul, in speaking to the Thessalonians and preparing them for the return of Jesus, describes the biblical nature of the "true church." He says that a true New Testament church:

- Is established by the preaching of the true gospel by sincere and effective Christian preachers.
- The true church's conduct and purity is continually being refined and challenged by the Holy Spirit.
- The true church is growing in the knowledge of spiritual things.

The Apostles never condemned any church for not growing in numerical size but often exhorted churches for not growing more pure in their conduct (I Corinthians) or growing in the knowledge of spiritual things (Galatians, Colossians, Hebrews). True churches are continually advancing in their knowledge of Christ and His teachings – especially in the serious preparation for His sure return one day.

In this chapter we will review Paul's teaching about the end times and how to prepare for them.

The Problem

> But we do not want you to be uninformed, brethren, about those who are asleep, so that you will not grieve as do the rest who have no hope.
> - I Thessalonians 4:13

It seems that the Thessalonians were worried about what would happen to those Christians who died before Jesus returned; they expected Jesus to return during their lifetime and when some of their number died they were confused and worried about what would happen to them. They were first generation Christians who had little teaching on this matter while Paul was with them.

Paul uses certain words that we need to note:

- Uninformed – without knowledge, ignorant
- Asleep – often used to represent death for Christians. It was used to signify a peaceful rest of a temporary nature which, for Christians, death was to be.

Paul didn't want them to react to the death of a Christian in the same way that non-Christians reacted to death. There were three main ways that pagans reacted to death:

1. **Ignore** – Pretend it won't really happen. Put it off. Refuse to discuss it or really deal with the eventuality of death. Majority of people do this.
2. **Deny** – Call it something else. Whole religions are built up around the idea that death isn't death but really a transformation of sorts. The idea is that they really don't

die – they live on through their children; absorbed into the greater consciousness; reincarnated into something else.

3. **Fear** – This is the reaction Paul is talking about here. The people of his generation knew death, and their only response was fear and grief because they had no hope beyond the grave.

But Paul wanted them to be informed concerning death and what eventually would happen to those who died as Christians. They shouldn't ignore, deny or fear death. They should open their eyes and see what exactly is going to happen to all Christians when they die or when the end of the world finally comes.

Gentiles have no hope but Christians do:

The Hope

> For if we believe that Jesus died and rose again, even so God will bring with Him those who have fallen asleep in Jesus.
> - I Thessalonians 4:14

Christians have hope for life after death because they have a historical precedent upon which they can base their faith: the resurrection of Jesus Christ. The basic promise that Jesus makes to His disciples is that if they believe/trust Him – what happened to Him after death will happen to them after death as well, a resurrection to a new life without death. Why? Because Jesus died without sin, death could not hold Him (Acts 2:24). When we become Christians we also die without sin (having been forgiven) and so death cannot hold us either. For this reason sin cannot hold us or turn us over to eternal condemnation.

Jesus was without sin because He didn't commit any. We are without sin because we are forgiven.

Paul is reassuring the Christians at Thessalonica that as sure as God raised Jesus from the dead, He will resurrect all of those who have died faithfully serving the Lord. There is no need to worry that they will be left behind, all who believed in Jesus will be raised by Jesus when He returns.

The Details – I Thessalonians 4:15-5:3

Paul now gives details as to what the Christian will experience at the end of the world. He does not, however, give details about:

- Resurrection of sinners – Matthew 25:31-32, Acts 24:15
- The judgment of the wicked – John 5:28-29
- What happens to the heavens and earth – II Peter 3:10-12
- Hell or punishment of sinners – II Thessalonians 1:9
- Kingdom given up to the Father – I Corinthians 15:24

This doesn't mean that these things are not happening at the same time ("...twinkling of an eye" I Corinthians 15:52), but Paul focuses his attention on what will happen to Christians at the end of the world when Jesus will return.

Paul confirms that the details he is about to teach them were taught to him directly by the Lord Himself concerning His return:

1. Some Christians will be alive and on earth when Jesus returns.

> For this we say to you by the word of the Lord, that we who are alive and remain until the coming of the Lord.
> - I Thessalonians 4:15a

2. These Christians will not go to heaven before the ones who are dead are resurrected.

> Will not precede those who have fallen asleep.
> - I Thessalonians 4:15b

3. The Lord will descend from heaven.

> For the Lord Himself will descend from heaven.
> - I Thessalonians 4:16a

4. These will be the signs of His appearance:

> With a shout, with the voice of the archangel and with the trumpet of God.
> - I Thessalonians 4:16b

- Shout
- Voice of an archangel
- Trumpet of God

These **could** all be symbolic ways of saying that Jesus' coming will be announced in such a way that no one will miss it.

5. The dead in Christ will be resurrected first.

> And the dead in Christ will rise first.
> - I Thessalonians 4:16c

This doesn't mean that at some later date sinners will be resurrected. Paul at this point is dealing only with Christians who are alive and those who are dead when Jesus comes. His point is that before the alive Christians go to be with Jesus, the dead Christians will first be resurrected. In a situation where many things will be happening simultaneously, Paul is concentrating on one specific thing: Christians and their experience at the end of the world.

6. The living and resurrected Christians will ascend into the clouds to be with Jesus.

> Then we who are alive and remain will be caught up together with them in the clouds to meet the Lord in the air
> - I Thessalonians 4:17a

In the same way Jesus ascended in a cloud to return to heaven, the living and resurrected Christians will ascend to be with Jesus in the sky.

7. This condition of being together with Jesus in the heavens (not on earth, no reign here on earth) will be the situation that will remain forever.

> and so we shall always be with the Lord.
> - I Thessalonians 4:17b

This knowledge concerning the end of time and death gives a Christian great comfort and confidence to face the end of life here on earth. Paul encourages them to use this teaching to encourage one another.

> Therefore comfort one another with these words.
> - I Thessalonians 4:18

8. No one knows for certain when Jesus will return, but it is certain that He will.

> Now as to the times and the epochs, brethren, you have no need of anything to be written to you. For you yourselves know full well that the day of the Lord will come just like a thief in the night. While they are saying, "Peace and safety!" then destruction will come upon them suddenly like labor pains upon a woman with child, and they will not escape.
> - I Thessalonians 5:1-3

There will even be some who are teaching peace and safety (just like the false prophets in the Old Testament who prophesied the security of Jerusalem when in reality it was on the verge of destruction). The destruction that will come at the end of the world for sinners will be sudden, without warning and complete; none will escape.

The Thessalonians were young Christians with a specific question about a complicated teaching – Paul gives them a focused, specific response without going into great detail.

Summary

1. Paul is adding to the knowledge of the Thessalonian church concerning the return of Jesus and the situation regarding those Christians who will already be dead when He comes.

2. Paul reassures them that their hope in Jesus based on His resurrection will be fulfilled in their own resurrection when He comes.

3. He gives the details concerning Jesus' return, focusing on what will happen to Christians specifically on the last day:

    - When Jesus returns the dead in Christ will be resurrected first.

    - Both living and resurrected Christians will ascend together to be with Jesus forever in heaven.

    - No one knows when this will happen, but it will happen and suddenly.

6.
8 WAYS TO BE READY

One thing that Paul describes in this epistle is that the true church has certain characteristics. And these do not have anything to do with size, age, wealth, building or staff. He sees the Thessalonian church as a true church because it experienced a true conversion at the hands of true and sincere ministers. In addition to this, it was growing in moral purity and knowledge of God's word, specifically – what would actually happen when Jesus returned.

In chapter 5 I explained that although many things happen simultaneously at Jesus' return (wicked judged / heaven and earth destroyed, etc.) Paul focuses only on what happens to Christians in his letter to the Thessalonians (dead Christians rise to join live Christians to be with Jesus in the air forever).

If these things are to be so, Paul explains to them how they can prepare for this sure event.

1. Watch Yourself – vs. 4-10

> But you, brethren, are not in darkness, that the day would overtake you like a thief; for you are all sons of light and sons of day. We are not of night nor of darkness;
> - I Thessalonians 5:4-5

Christians are in the light (they see what is coming) not like unbelievers who are not aware that their end is near (they're in the dark). He talks about this watchfulness.

> So then let us not sleep as others do, but let us be alert and sober.
> - I Thessalonians 5:6

- Alert (watching / paying attention)
- Sober (peaceful and clear minded)

> For those who sleep do their sleeping at night, and those who get drunk get drunk at night. But since we are of the day, let us be sober, having put on the breastplate of faith and love, and as a helmet, the hope of salvation.
> - I Thessalonians 5:7-8

Our sobriety is spiritual in nature and distinguishes itself in that we live by faith in Christ, love for others and a firm hope that Jesus will come. We don't allow ourselves to be led away (inebriated) by the sin in this world of faithlessness, hard heartedness and loss of hope for eternal life. This is spiritual drunkenness.

> For God has not destined us for wrath, but for obtaining salvation through our Lord Jesus Christ, who died for us, so that whether we are awake or asleep, we will live together with Him.
> - I Thessalonians 5:9-10

Paul encourages them to be watchful against spiritual laziness and sin because they are destined for eternal life with Jesus, not punishment, and they need to keep alert so they won't lose their way. People lose their way because they are careless with their faith. Paul says to watch (pay attention) and be alert as well as sober-minded in spiritual matters in order to be ready when Christ comes.

Another thing he mentions in order to prepare...

2. Build up the Church – vs. 11

> Therefore encourage one another and build up one another, just as you also are doing.
> - I Thessalonians 5:11

Paul uses two key words to describe our ministry one to another in the church.

1. **Encourage** (comfort, exhort). This is the same word used by Jesus in John 16:7 in referring to the Holy Spirit. It means to call to one side. The idea is to support someone else in weakness.

2. **Build-up** (edify). This word originally meant to build a home. It means to promote spiritual growth in another. This is done by teaching, example and encouragement that is patiently given to those who need such things.

Note that Paul says that the individual members are to comfort and edify each other. This is different than the common notion of the preacher being responsible for doing this for the entire church. Many times members get angry and disappointed in him if he fails us.

Our activity in the church either builds the church or tears it down – Paul says that a ready Christian is one the Lord finds building the church when He appears. This, he says, is the responsibility of the entire church, not just the minister.

3. Respect Your Leaders – vs. 12-13a

> But we request of you, brethren, that you appreciate those who diligently labor among you, and have

> charge over you in the Lord and give you instruction, and that you esteem them very highly in love because of their work.
> - I Thessalonians 5:12-13a

Paul refers to the work of the leaders and the attitude the church should have towards them:

1. Leaders fulfill their ministries if they are working hard (Greek word for trial) in their roles:
   - Serving (not just decision making)
   - Teaching (not just talking)
   - Training (not just supervising)
2. The church needs to recognize that this is the work that leaders are doing and ought to appreciate them for doing it because it is being done for them. The best way to encourage leaders in the church is to love them and cooperate with them:
   - Serving by their side (not under)
   - Obeying their teaching (if it is Biblical)
   - Accept the training with enthusiasm

A church is not ready for the return of its Lord if it is complaining and not cooperating with its leaders; and the leaders are not ready if they are not working hard in their ministries.

4. Be at Peace with one Another – vs. 13b-15

> Live in peace with one another. We urge you, brethren,

> admonish the unruly, encourage the fainthearted, help the weak, be patient with everyone. See that no one repays another with evil for evil, but always seek after that which is good for one another and for all people.
> - I Thessalonians 5:13b-15

Paul states the objective then explains the method:

- Admonish the unruly (warn troublemakers). In Thessalonica there were some who did not work and caused trouble in the church.
- Encourage the fainthearted (discouraged). Encourage not to give up for those who were not strong in the faith.
- Help the weak (weak to temptation). Hold on to those who are easily drawn away from the truth, purity, etc.
- Be patient (with everyone). Be ready to "bear under" all people who you come in contact with.
- Return good for evil (Christian reaction). To those who offend us we offer the other cheek, not the fist. (It is to a man's glory to overlook a transgression, Proverbs 19:11.)

When there are disputes in the church it is usually because we violate these principles. We cannot be happy when Jesus returns if He finds us divided and at war with one another or ignoring one another's spiritual needs.

5. Rejoice Always – vs. 16

> Rejoice always;
> - I Thessalonians 5:16

This seems like an impossible thing considering the hardships of life, but Paul is writing with a view of the return of Jesus. Regardless of our circumstances we can always rejoice because nothing can change the fact that Jesus will return and when He does we will be with Him. How happy I will be if the Lord comes and finds me rejoicing.

6. Pray Always – vs. 17-18

> Pray without ceasing; in everything give thanks; for this is God's will for you in Christ Jesus.
> - I Thessalonians 5:17-18

A Christian isn't always praying (he needs to sleep) but he can always pray if he wants to. Why? The reasons for giving thanks are endless:

- It is God's will that he pray.
- Jesus is always present as our mediator.
- The Holy Spirit is always there to help our weakness in prayer.

A ready church is a church with an open communication line with God through prayer. Wouldn't it be great to be in the middle of prayer when Jesus comes?

7. Study the Word – vs. 19-21

> Do not quench the Spirit; do not despise prophetic utterances. But examine everything carefully; hold fast to that which is good;
> - I Thessalonians 5:19-21

Paul teaches them how to respond to those teaching them the word through the gift of prophetic utterance. They are to listen (not to ignore these prophets) but they are to test (examine) carefully what they say and hold on (do) that which is good (teaching). Today we don't have prophets, we have the Bible that provides us with God's word, but the admonition is the same: we are to be doers of the word, not just hearers.

Jesus said that when He returns it will not be the ones who say "Lord, Lord" who will enter in but those who do the will of the Father.

8. Be Pure – vs. 22

> Abstain from every form of evil.
> - I Thessalonians 5:22

Notice that Paul says every form of evil. This not only includes moral evil (adultery, drunkenness, dishonesty) but also spiritual evil such as false religions and human philosophies that deny God.

When a bride prepares for her wedding she doesn't go out on a date the night before the wedding or begin cleaning out the garage. Why? She wants to remain devoted and clean for her future husband. The church is the bride of Christ and is ready for His coming if she is completely devoted to only Him and remains pure.

This is not meant to be an exhaustive list, but if you do these to prepare they will lead you into all other good works.

Why do we need to be ready?

> Now may the God of peace Himself sanctify you
> entirely; and may your spirit and soul and body be

> preserved complete, without blame at the coming of our Lord Jesus Christ. Faithful is He who calls you, and He also will bring it to pass.
> - I Thessalonians 5:23-24

We need to be ready because God promises that He will do His part which is to completely perfect us in the twinkling of an eye when Jesus returns, and that day will come because God Himself has promised (and which of His promises has He ever failed to accomplish so far?).

Why is Paul teaching this?

> Brethren, pray for us. Greet all the brethren with a holy kiss. I adjure you by the Lord to have this letter read to all the brethren. The grace of our Lord Jesus Christ be with you.
> - I Thessalonians 5:25-28

Paul ends his first letter with a salutation, request for prayers and a blessing. He also commits them to reading his epistle to the church so that everyone would be ready should Jesus come in their lifetimes.

Summary

If you remember anything about Paul's first letter to the Thessalonians it is this:

- One day you are going to see Jesus Christ.

When you are discouraged, saddened or suffering:

- Because you are lonely
- Because you are sick

- Because you don't have enough time, talent, etc.
- Because you are failing to accomplish all that you ought or want to do.

Just remember that in one brief moment it will all be over and you will actually see the one you prayed to and trusted for your eternal life.

Therefore:

- Watch yourselves
- Build up one another
- Respect your leaders
- Be at peace with each other
- Rejoice and pray always
- Study carefully the word
- Remain as pure as you can be…

...so that you will be ready when Jesus comes for you.

7.
INTRODUCTION TO II THESSALONIANS

In 51 AD Paul the Apostle established a congregation of the church in the city of Thessalonica. This young assembly had to survive in a port city that was rich, influential and pagan. Soon after, Paul was driven out of town by Jewish religious leaders and eventually made his way to Corinth in southern Greece.

After a while he received a report from Timothy, a young evangelist that worked with him, concerning the progress of the young church at Thessalonica. Paul responds to this news by writing two letters. In the first letter he does four things:

- He expresses joy at their faithfulness in persevering in trials and adversity.
- He defends his conduct against charges that he was a fake and opportunist.
- He encourages them not to lose faith and continue serving God.
- He teaches them about the second coming of Christ and how they should conduct themselves in the meantime.

In our study of I Thessalonians we have seen that Paul, among other things, described the true church and what that church looked and acted like. Basically, Paul said that the true church:

- Began with a true conversion - the true gospel was being preached.

- True ministers ministered to it - ministers who conducted themselves in a holy way.
- Had true spiritual growth - the true church acted like the church.
- Was pure in all things.
- Grew in knowledge continually.
- Was ready for the return of Christ.

In the second letter, which we begin to examine in this chapter, Paul continues in his praise of the Thessalonians and provides more information concerning the second coming as well as an admonition to the church to deal with disorderly members.

Note that like his other epistles this one is neatly organized and broken into three clear areas of material.

1. Encouragement – 1:1-12
2. Education – 2:1-12
3. Exhortation – 3:1-15

Encouragement – II Thessalonians 1:1-12

Salutation – vs. 1-2

> Paul and Silvanus and Timothy, to the church of the Thessalonians in God our Father and the Lord Jesus Christ: Grace to you and peace from God the Father and the Lord Jesus Christ.
> - II Thessalonians 1:1-2

This is where we find "internal" evidence for Paul as the author of these letters. External evidences are things like references about Paul's authorship in other documents written at the same period of time.

Note that Jesus' name is put in the same divine position as God: the one who gives grace and power.

The point is that the only combination that can produce grace and peace is the relationship between God and His church in Christ.

Thanksgiving – vs. 3-4

> We ought always to give thanks to God for you, brethren, as is only fitting, because your faith is greatly enlarged, and the love of each one of you toward one another grows ever greater; therefore, we ourselves speak proudly of you among the churches of God for your perseverance and faith in the midst of all your persecutions and afflictions which you endure.
> - II Thessalonians 1:3-4

Paul thanks God not for what they have given to him but for who and what they are becoming in Christ. They are growing in strength, faith and love despite their persecutions.

Paul expresses the joy of every father or farmer or inventor or artist or teacher who sees the product of his work and training being admired and approved by others.

This is the true reward of mature Christians: seeing younger Christians whom they have mentored and led grow in Christ. It's also the most painful and frustrating.

Of course you cannot know the joy or the pain if you've never invested yourself in the growth and development of another person. The surest way to grow in joy and Christian love is to invest in the development of another.

The Righteous Judgment of God – vs. 5-10

> This is a plain indication of God's righteous judgment so that you will be considered worthy of the kingdom of God, for which indeed you are suffering.
> - II Thessalonians 1:5

Paul now addresses the sufferings that the Thessalonians are experiencing and God's righteous judgment concerning it. Some of their trials stemmed from:

- The pagan society they lived in was hostile.
- The Jewish leaders who harassed them.
- The false teachers that had crept in among them.
- The constant temptation by Satan to quit and to go back into the world.

Note that their trials and challenges to their faith are not much different than what we experience today in our time and in our culture. Paul talks about "righteous judgment."

- Judgment = separation and decision
- Righteous = a decision without any prejudice or malice

Paul comforts them in their suffering by telling them that:

1. Their suffering and their perseverance through it serves the greater good of helping to establish the church. There is a cost attached to establishing the Kingdom of God on earth. It began with Christ's

suffering and continues in each generation with the sufferings of the church to remain faithful and pure. We need to remember this when we suffer in some way in order to serve the church.

2. He tells them that God not only permits them to suffer on behalf of the church, He also helps the church endure. Remember that God's answer to Paul when he cried out to be relieved of his thorn in the flesh; God answered by giving him the ability to endure it, He didn't take it away.

3. He tells them that God will punish later those who are making trouble now. These and the wicked will suffer later and the believers will find relief and rest later.

Paul also gives details concerning the punishment of the wicked in this epistle. In I Thessalonians he talks about what happens to the living and "sleeping" saints when Jesus returns. In II Thessalonians he talks about what will happen to the unfaithful and wicked when Jesus returns.

> For after all it is only just for God to repay with affliction those who afflict you,
> - II Thessalonians 1:6

He will repay those who afflicted Christians and made them suffer. See Romans 12:19 *"Revenge is mine…"*

> and to give relief to you who are afflicted and to us as well when the Lord Jesus will be revealed from heaven with His mighty angels in flaming fire,
> - II Thessalonians 1:7

Christ will come from heaven with angels and fire. Angels to announce His coming and glory, fire to fulfill His judgment against the wicked.

> Dealing out retribution to those who do not know God and to those who do not obey the gospel of our Lord Jesus. These will pay the penalty of eternal destruction, away from the presence of the Lord and from the glory of His power.
> - II Thessalonians 1:8-9

Those who do not know God and those who do not obey the gospel are the same. These will suffer eternal destruction or punishment away from God. This is by God's decree and is a just punishment. People who say God is unfair are mistaken. To be deprived of the sight of the Lord will be the substance of the punishment and it will be eternal.

> When He comes to be glorified in His saints on that day, and to be marveled at among all who have believed – for our testimony to you was believed.
> - II Thessalonians 1:10

All of this will happen when Jesus comes. The believers will reflect His glory (glorified, resurrected bodies). Believers will rejoice and marvel at His presence because they were faithful in their belief. The rest (unbelievers, wicked) will be banished from His presence. All of this happens at once, in the "twinkling of an eye."

Prayer – vs. 11-12

> To this end also we pray for you always, that our God will count you worthy of your calling, and fulfill every desire for goodness and the work of faith with power, so that the name of our Lord Jesus will be glorified in you, and you in Him, according to the grace of our God and the Lord Jesus Christ.
> - II Thessalonians 1:11-12

Paul continues with his constant prayer for them. His prayer request, however, is very specific.

- That God complete the work that He began in them.
- That He finish the thing that He originally called them for through the gospel.
- God calls us, through the gospel, to separate ourselves from this world and begin to follow and become like His Son Jesus Christ.

We begin on this road of change and transformation when we respond to the gospel with faith and we express that faith in repentance and baptism (Acts 2:38). This initial event changes us from lost to saved; condemned to justified; outcast to son/daughter; prisoner of sin to free from sin and death.

Another thing begins to happen to us at this moment as well: we receive the Holy Spirit to dwell within us. Through the influence of the Holy Spirit, God's word and the church we also begin a process of growth, development and maturity called sanctification. Paul refers to this phenomenon when he prays that the "work," the work of sanctification, will be completed when Jesus returns.

When Jesus returns we will shed our mortal bodies and be filled with a body that is able to exist in the spiritual world. Some people have questions about cremation because of the resurrection. At the resurrection we won't be taking back our old flesh, no matter what condition or place that it's in (the ground, the sea or an urn).

Paul prays that in the meantime, until Jesus returns, this mutual honor continue. Christians honor God with their faith and good works until Jesus returns. God blessed man by helping to mature and grow in Christ until the day comes when they will be perfectly like Him with their resurrection and glorification. This reciprocal blessing should continue until Christ returns and the process of sanctification will be complete. And the process will be complete when sinners will be judged once for all and saints will be brought to heaven once and for all time.

Summary

Paul begins his second letter to this young church by encouraging them to persevere in faithfulness to the word, loving kindness to one another and a firm hope of their reward. He does this by reminding them of one major idea: one day God will bring His judgment on all men. Those who remain faithful will be rewarded and those who don't or reject the truth will be punished. And the reward will be a wonderful reward, a reward worth waiting for. And the punishment will be a frightening thing, a punishment worth avoiding.

Exhortation

If you look around, you do see injustice and wickedness in this world. You don't have to look far to see lazy people and hypocrites in the church. These may be good excuses to get angry or discouraged and walk away from God and His church; but these types of excuses only work if you are looking at and taking the short view. In the long view (which is God's view) all wrongs will be righted, all liars revealed, all the lazy and hypocrites exposed and all the faithful ones rewarded. Our work as Christians is not to judge, punish or decide; these are God's prerogatives. Our job is to make sure that we are faithful in our lives and witness so that we can share in the glorious witness of Christ when He comes. Let's never forget that there will be both reward and punishment.

8.
EVENTS BEFORE THE LAST DAY

I and II Thessalonians are two letters that Paul wrote to a young church that he established in 51 AD. The key ideas he writes about are:

1. His joy over the fact that despite their many trials and persecutions, this young church was persevering in faithfulness, knowledge and brotherly love, and preparing for the return of Christ.

2. The other things he writes about are the events surrounding the return of Jesus. In his first letter he describes what will happen to Christians (living and dead) when Jesus returns and he exhorts them to be ready. In the second letter he explains what's going to happen to sinners and the unfaithful when Jesus appears again. He encourages them by telling them not be disheartened by what the wicked are doing; when He comes, Jesus will reward and punish according to a person's deeds. After this, Paul continues his letter by instructing them concerning the events that will take place prior to Jesus' return.

The day has not come – 2:1-2

> Now we request you, brethren, with regard to the coming of our Lord Jesus Christ and our gathering together to Him, that you not be quickly shaken from your composure or be disturbed either by a spirit or a message or a letter as if from us, to the effect that the day of the Lord has come.
> - II Thessalonians 2:1-2

If you read between the lines, it seems that this was the core problem of this church. Someone may have claimed to have a prophecy, an authority or a teaching from an Apostle claiming that the second coming had already occurred. Someone may have promoted the idea that they were already in the midst of it or that it was very near. The effect on the church was disturbing. It seems that they were becoming spiritually unbalanced, agitated and confused.

Paul begs them not to lose their composure and become overly disturbed with this teaching and false notions.

Whatever its source, he discounts it and reaffirms that before the "day of the Lord" comes, other significant events must take place first, and he goes on to give details about these events.

Language / Literary Style - vs. 3-12

The next passage is among the most difficult in the Bible. Even Peter the Apostle attests to the fact that some of Paul's writings are difficult to discern (II Peter 3:15-16). In addition to the complicated ideas to grasp, this section is written in a literary style that is impossible to understand unless we have some background on the terms used.

Apocalyptic

This passage was written in the apocalyptic literary style that was filled with symbolic words and images. The word apocalyptic means "uncovering" or a "revealing." It was a style of writing used by many in the ancient world including prophets and other Old Testament writers to describe in dramatic terms the content of their prophecies. They also used this type of language to warn the nations about impending war or judgment from God.

- Daniel 7:13 – Dreams
- Ezekiel 32:2 – Visions

- Joel, Acts 2:19-20 – Prophecy

The apocalyptic style was mainly used in times of trouble or at those periods when the Jews were being oppressed. In many instances the writing was understandable only to the Jews, but not to others because of the symbols that had meaning only to a Jew. This style was also used by the New Testament writers for the same reasons.

- Jesus (Matthew 24:1-34) – Destruction of Jerusalem
- Paul (II Thessalonians) – Apostasy and second coming
- John, Revelation – Destruction of Rome and the judgment

The thing to remember is that when this style is used it is a "coded" message to the reader. It may be disturbing to read, but was actually meant to comfort and encourage God's people in times of trouble. At other times it was to warn or point to events that would take place in the future, all with the use of symbols.

This is the language Paul switches to in II Thessalonians 2:3-8. We cannot discern his message unless we understand the symbolism in which the message was written.

Symbols / Terms - vs. 3-8

> 3 Let no one in any way deceive you, for it will not come unless the apostasy comes first, and the man of lawlessness is revealed, the son of destruction, 4 who opposes and exalts himself above every so-called god or object of worship, so that he takes his seat in the temple of God, displaying himself as being God. 5 Do you not remember that while I was still with you, I was telling you these things? 6 And you know what restrains him now, so that in his time he will be revealed. 7 For the mystery of lawlessness is already at work; only he who now restrains will do so until he is

> taken out of the way. [8] Then that lawless one will be revealed whom the Lord will slay with the breath of His mouth and bring to an end by the appearance of His coming;
> - II Thessalonians 2:3-8

Before we search for over-all meaning, let's look at some of the key terms:

1. Apostasy (rebellion) – vs. 3

Literally means to fall away. In this case it means to fall away from Christ and His teachings. Apostasy in the New Testament refers only to the Christian faith. For example, Muslims cannot be apostate because they are never in the faith to begin with. We can refer to non-believers as pagans or the lost, but for Christians who go away from Christ or His teachings, the correct term is to be an apostate or in apostasy.

2. Man of Lawlessness / Son of Destruction – vs. 3

Lawlessness means sin or sinfulness. The sin that accompanies the apostasy. This is a one-of-a-kind, unique personality, power or organization that embodies the sin. Man of Lawlessness; Son of Destruction; Perdition; Antichrist – all refer to the same thing.

3. Restraining Influence – vs. 6

The person or power that restrains the Man of Lawlessness (whatever form it takes) from declaring his/its position or revealing himself.

4. Mystery of Lawlessness – vs. 7

This refers to the actual outworking of evil generated by the apostasy. Just like the outworking of good caused by the word of God in building the Kingdom can be seen in good works and conduct, the apostasy also spreads its influence in a negative way (leaven).

5. Breath of His Mouth - vs. 8

The word of God, the Scriptures (Revelation 2:16).

6. Appearance of His Coming - vs. 8

The second coming or return of Christ.

7. Prophecy

Paul is prophesying here based on the revelation from God given to him. He is telling them what will happen in the future and at the end of time. This is the same thing as when he described what will happen to the faithful and the wicked at the end. One thing to note in order to avoid confusion, however, is that prophecy gives the facts of what will happen and the succession of events but it rarely gives the time of, or in between, these events. So, we know what is going to take place and the order of things but are not told when they will happen, how much time elapses between the events or when all the events will be completed.

For example, John the Baptist prophesied the coming of the Messiah as well as the judgment of the Jewish nation (Matthew 3:11-12). In his mind these two events were to happen at the same time. This is why when he was imprisoned by Herod, he sent disciples to Jesus to inquire if Jesus was truly the Messiah (Matthew 11:2-3). He was confused because Jesus the Messiah was here but there were no signs of judgment on the nation. Thirty seven years after Jesus' death and resurrection however, and some 40 years after John's death at the hands of Herod – God's judgment on Jerusalem, spoken of by John, came down on the city in the form of a Roman army. In 70 AD the nation of Israel came to an end as the Roman army destroyed the city and killed most of its people – John's prophecy fulfilled. John understood the events and the sequence correctly but did not know the time in between these events.

In the passage in II Thessalonians we see Paul predicting events that will happen in the future and he explains the sequence of these events but not their time frame. It could have all happened during their lifetimes in the first century or take 10,000 years to fulfill. It will all happen in the sequence that it has been spoken of, but only God knows when. When we study this passage therefore, we are studying the meaning and sequence of what will take place but have no idea of the time frame.

Sequence of Events – vs. 3-12

Paul explains two major events that must take place before the return of Christ. He explains this in order to calm their fears in thinking that the return of Christ has already happened and they missed it; or that it was to happen very soon.

1. The Apostasy – vs. 3a

The return of Jesus does not happen until this takes place. The Apostasy is a rebellion, a falling away from faith in Christ and obedience to His word. This is an event that takes place within Christianity! Paul mentions that this apostasy was inevitable and likely within his lifetime.

> Be on guard for yourselves and for all the flock, among which the Holy Spirit has made you overseers, to shepherd the church of God which He purchased with his own blood. I know that after my departure savage wolves will come in among you, not sparing the flock; and from among your own selves men will arise, speaking perverse things, to draw away the disciples after them.
> - Acts 20:28-30

> For the time will come when they will not endure sound doctrine; but wanting to have their ears tickled, they will accumulate for themselves teachers in accordance to their own desires, and will turn away their ears from the truth and will turn aside to myths.
> - II Timothy 4:3-4

Apostasy is the action of leaving the truth and embracing a lie. It is the love of what is not true and the ultimate cause of condemnation. The apostasy began in the first century as teachers rose up to deny the divinity of Christ and continue to this day as many "Christian" groups deny the inspiration of the Scriptures and teach that Christ is an angel (Jehovah Witnesses) or a man who became a god (Mormons).

2. The Man of Lawlessness is Revealed – vs. 3-7

The big question here is, "What is he like?"

Vs. 3 – One of a kind person or personage could be embodied in a personality, organization, philosophy or movement (i.e. Hitler – Nazism). Hidden at first, then revealed.

Vs. 4 – Opposes every god or object of worship. Does not deny that there is a God, but opposes every form of deity. Takes God's place within God's sanctuary or God's dwelling place. Places himself where God is and makes himself equal with God within Christianity. God's sanctuary on earth is within the hearts and minds of His people.

Vs. 5-7 – His influence is manifested before he is. Like a seed develops roots, stalk and leaves before it blooms; he will develop an evil influence and with time will mature to manifest himself for who and what he truly is: the Man of Lawlessness, the Son of Destruction, the Antichrist. Now Paul says that his influence is (was) being restrained at the time Paul wrote his letters to the Thessalonians. It had not bloomed yet but was already at work in its evil influence. This manifestation, he says, was being restrained by a person or power or a combination of both which will later be removed.

What will the Man of Lawlessness do?

Vs. 9-13 – He will deceive people in the name of God and Christ in order to seduce them to believe what is false and be lost because of it. He will do this using all manner of false power, false signs, false wonders, wicked lies and deceptions. These powerful weapons are necessary to convince people that the lie is true. He will know that he is a liar, he will lie on purpose and will do so in order to destroy the souls of men (vs. 10). Paul tells us in advance why Christians will believe these lies:

- They don't love the truth, they love sin, love the world, love self, but not the truth (like John 3:19).

- God gives them what they desire (lies) by allowing the Man of Lawlessness to work his works so that those among the believers who love lies will get their fill. The "deluding influence" is the cumulative effect produced by believing error/lies. God doesn't send lies or error, He permits and directs where Satan may work (i.e. Job – Satan needed permission to attack him).

- People who love wickedness eventually refuse to listen, or accept truth and they will have ample time to demonstrate their evil and error so as to also demonstrate how just God is in condemning and punishing them.

What will happen to him?

Vs. 8 – God will destroy him in two steps: the breath of His mouth – the word of truth; and the appearance of His son – the return of Christ for the judgment of all liars.

Remember that all these events will take place but we don't know when or if they will take place all at once or be spread out over a period of time.

Summary

Paul tells the Thessalonian church that the "Day of the Lord" has not come so they shouldn't be worried or upset by anyone who brings a teaching to the contrary. He tells them that before the Lord returns two important things must happen.

- The Apostasy must occur and had already begun in some aspects.
- The Man of Lawlessness had to be revealed for who he is.

In the next chapter we're to examine several theories explaining who the "Man of Lawlessness" really is, how he works today and what the "restraining power" might be (there are four possibilities). In the meantime there are three very practical lessons we can learn from the material we have just covered:

1. Bad teaching hurts the church.

We need to be careful not only of how we live, but also what we teach. The only way to avoid false teaching is to continually stay with Christ's teaching and make corrections when there is error. Bad teaching, careless teaching, teaching of worldly ideas instead of Biblical concepts often divides the church or slows its growth.

2. Satan desires to destroy souls.

Our prayers, our watchfulness, our faithfulness to God and His word are what protect us. Note that it is the word wielded by Christ Himself that destroys Satan in the end.

3. We can be the true church.

The right and true religion and the church that practices it is the one that carefully and humbly follows Christ's teaching. Don't be fooled by appearances, signs, flashiness – the word of God is our only sure sign. Our job is not to judge if other churches or groups are legitimate or not, that judgment belongs to God; our task is to follow God's word and encourage others to do the same.

9. WHO IS THE MAN OF LAWLESSNESS

These letters contain two major ideas:

1. Thanksgiving for the faithfulness and perseverance of this young church in the face of adversity.

2. Important teaching concerning the return of Christ.

The first letter contained information about the actual return of Christ and what would happen to believers of that time. The second letter describes key events that must take place before the return of the Lord. This was necessary teaching because there were some who had begun to say that Christ had already come or His coming was imminent.

In his second letter Paul reassures them that the "day" had not yet come because other events had to take place first:

- The Apostasy – the falling away of believers from the truth.

- The revelation of the Man of Lawlessness as his restraining influence is removed.

Previously, I said that the falling away from the teachings of Christ had already begun. In this chapter we are going to look at the possible identification of the Man of Lawlessness and his restraining influence.

> Now we request you, brethren, with regard to the coming of our Lord Jesus Christ and our gathering together to Him, that you not be quickly shaken from your composure or be disturbed either by a spirit or a

> message or a letter as if from us, to the effect that the day of the Lord has come. Let no one in any way deceive you, for it will not come unless the apostasy comes first, and the man of lawlessness is revealed, the son of destruction, who opposes and exalts himself above every so-called god or object of worship, so that he takes his seat in the temple of God, displaying himself as being God. Do you not remember that while I was still with you, I was telling you these things? And you know what restrains him now, so that in his time he will be revealed. For the mystery of lawlessness is already at work; only he who now restrains will do so until he is taken out of the way. Then that lawless one will be revealed whom the Lord will slay with the breath of His mouth and bring to an end by the appearance of His coming; that is, the one whose coming is in accord with the activity of Satan, with all power and signs and false wonders, and with all the deception of wickedness for those who perish, because they did not receive the love of the truth so as to be saved.
> - II Thessalonians 2:1-10

There have been several theories about who or what the Man of Lawlessness might be. Let's review the 4 main ones:

1. The Roman Empire

It's easy to see why early Christians might think that the Roman Empire was the Man of Lawlessness.

- It opposed Christianity
- It demanded worship of the emperor as god
- It promoted great evil

The restraining power was thought to be the actual Roman government which kept the emperor's power in check. This theory falls apart however, because the Scripture says that the Man of Lawlessness would be there, even at the end, and be destroyed by Jesus' coming. The Roman Empire and her emperors are long gone and so cannot fulfill this portion of Paul's prophecy.

2. Satan

Some think that Satan himself is the Man of Lawlessness. The idea is that he works behind the scenes to create and promote evil, and then one day actually becomes human in some form in order to personify the Man of Lawlessness. Many popular movies have used this idea (The Exorcist, Damien, Rosemary's Baby, Devil's Advocate).

In this theory, the Holy Spirit (perhaps working through the Word) is the restraining influence. The theory is that the Holy Spirit will be removed at the end so Satan can take human form and be destroyed by Jesus before he takes over the world.

There are some problems with this explanation as well:

- Verse 9 says that Satan is directing this person. Satan does not divide himself.
- There is no indication that the Holy Spirit is ever restrained by anyone other than an individual sinful Christian.
- No one can restrain the Holy Spirit's power working in someone else's life.
- Revelation 20:1-3 shows that Satan in being restrained for 1,000 years (The New Testament period) and the agent of that restraining power is an angel (not the Holy Spirit).
- Before the coming of Christ, Satan deceives the world with great power. After the cross and the gospel is preached, Satan's power is much diminished.

Therefore, something else (through Satan's remaining power) and someone else (manipulated by him) will manifest himself. The fact that he will be released suggests a great release of evil power present at the end, just before Jesus returns.

3. The Papacy

The institution of the papacy within Christianity fits well with the activity of the apostasy and the idea of the Man of Lawlessness. It is a favorite theory of evangelicals and extreme fundamentalists. Some of the pluses for this theory:

- It happens within Christianity and it is very visible.
- It grew out of the roots of apostasy sown in the first and second centuries.

The reorganization of the New Testament church from a local, autonomous, pastoral system to a model of organization based on the Roman hierarchical system produced four things that eventually damaged the church.

- The separation of ministers from laity and making them the special intermediaries between God and the church created a class system within the church. In a church based solely on the teachings of the New Testament, every member is a priest (Revelation 1:6); every member has a gift or ministry (Romans12:1-ff). This Biblical idea was replaced with an elitist view of ministry by the Roman Catholic Church.
- The papacy and its reorganization of the church gave special authority to pastors/elders over and above the local congregation and set into motion the pyramidal power system that exists in the Roman Catholic Church today. The Bible gives leadership to a group of elders for only one congregation. There is no authority in the church beyond the local level according to the New Testament.

- This reorganization under the Pope introduced new church positions and roles not found in Scriptures. Offices such as arch-bishop, cardinals, or popes were inventions of men, not authorized by Scripture which only recognizes the roles of:

    1. **Evangelist** (proclaimer)
        - Preacher/Apostle (missionary)
        - Minister (of the Gospel)
    2. **Deacon** (minister of work) Ephesians 4:11ff
    3. **Elder** (ministry of leadership)
        - Bishop/pastor/presbyter/overseer
    4. **Teacher** (minister of the Word)

    There are no other roles or offices in the church described in the New Testament.

- This reorganization put into the hands of men, boards and committees, the right to change, add or subtract from the teachings of Christ. Some of the changes over the years:

    - Infant baptism – Third century
    - Confessional – Fourth century
    - Transubstantiation – Ninth century
    - Indulgences – Fifteenth century
    - Infallibility – 1870

Just to name a few in the past.

The latest addition being promoted by the previous Pope is the doctrine of the Co-Mediatrix of Mary. This idea states that through her suffering, Mary the mother of Jesus, contributes to the sacrifice of Jesus on the cross for our sins. In other words, we're saved by the atoning work of Jesus and Mary.

In addition to these things, the papacy as the Man of Lawlessness also has other points that support this view. It claims superiority over every believer and demands obedience. It makes itself equal with God in the sense that the papacy claims infallibility in matters of teaching and condemns all those who oppose the Pope. It has consistently produced false doctrine, false miracles, elevated ordinary people to a semi-godlike role of "saint" in an effort to maintain rulership and credibility with its followers – and all done in the name of Christ.

The role of the papacy is the largest and longest unbroken apostasy visible within Christianity.

Some also think that the restraining influence over the papacy is the Roman Catholic Church structure, which has historically fought with the papacy (something like the struggle for power between the individual states and the federal government in the American political system). A good example of this conflict was seen when many in the college of bishops fought hard against the introduction of the doctrine of papal infallibility in 1870 but lost the battle when it was outvoted.

Others teach that the Reformation and the resulting spread of the Bible into the hands of common people has mortally wounded the papacy and that because of this it no longer has the power it once had. The idea is that the Reformation was the "breath of His mouth" that God sent to strike down the Man of Lawlessness = Papacy. Only the return of Jesus is left to completely discredit and destroy this institution.

Many scholars hold to this view concerning the papacy as the Man of Lawlessness. It is true that there are many parallels here and a good argument can be made, but let's also look at some of the problems with this teaching:

1. The Pope doesn't claim deity. He only claims authority in religious matters. At the moment he is trying to unite all religions and foster greater unity between Roman Catholics and Protestants.

2. In II Thessalonians the Apostasy is such that the Man of Lawlessness and the system he fosters is in open rebellion against Christ and the Gospel. Whatever its mistakes the Roman Catholic Church promotes belief in the God of the Bible, faith in Christ as well as high moral standards. It may have error in its teaching and practice, but many other groups who confess Christ have errors as well.

In the end I believe that the Roman Catholic system and the papacy are part of the Apostasy and they suffer from the delusions and errors brought about by the Man of Lawlessness. They are unwitting tools in the larger scheme of evil that creates confusion and heresy within Christianity – but they and the Pope are not the Man of Lawlessness as some believe and teach.

The apostasy is something that happens within Christianity and my opinion is that different unbiblical forms of Christianity practiced today (including Roman Catholicism, Mormonism, Seventh Day Adventism) are all individual parts of a general apostasy that began in the second century and continue today in different forms.

It is inaccurate, however, to say that the Man of Lawlessness is the head or leader of the Apostasy. The Apostasy begins and develops in many ways and then the Man of Lawlessness is revealed, as a separate event. These are separate things happening concurrently.

The Bible does not say that the Man of Lawlessness is a "religious" figure. In my opinion, this is the main reason why teaching that the Pope is the Man of Lawlessness is incorrect. Paul says that this figure opposes religion, opposes God, opposes worship and tries to take God's place as ruler over men.

Although this theory fits in many ways, the Pope and Roman Catholicism as the Man of Lawlessness do not match important facts the Bible gives about him.

4. A Principle of Lawlessness

One last possibility is that the Man of Lawlessness is the "principle" of evil and rebellion working in the world and manifesting itself in a variety of people and movements throughout history. You see the principle of lawlessness working in:

- The Roman Empire
- Barbarian wars
- Dark Ages
- Nazism/Communism
- Godless philosophy
- Fanatic religious aggression

These and other movements have tried to rule men without respect to God, or the God of the Bible. They have used lies, power and every evil device to achieve their goals. All have been caught up in the power of delusion caused by atheistic philosophy or the twisted religion of each age. In addition to these, every age produces a new version or face of this evil principle. We have witnessed several reincarnations in just the last two centuries:

- Materialism of the nineteenth century
- Humanism of the twentieth century
- Post Modernism of the twenty-first century

- Religious fanaticism of our day

All have opposed God, tried to destroy true worship, tried to take God's place in His own temple, which is the human heart.

This principle of evil (like yeast, working but not being seen) will continue working in this way until it is embodied in one person or one movement which will be more powerful, more evil and more threatening to man's soul than ever before.

The Man of Lawlessness will pose a threat because his revealing will be accompanied by:

- Personal claims to Deity
- Signs and wonders
- Visibility on a world-wide scale

The understanding that it is the Man of Lawlessness that is being revealed will be the sign that the return of Christ will be imminent. Remember: Jesus doesn't return until the Man of Lawlessness is revealed. Revealed to whom? To Christians of course!

Disbelievers and the wicked will not recognize him for who he is. Jesus promises that Christians will know; how? Jesus will reveal him to us, we don't have to worry that we won't see it or miss it. The Man of Lawlessness is revealed, he doesn't reveal himself.

Now, the restraining power that holds him back (verses 6-7) is referred to as a person and a power and himself a mystery. This restraining power could be the opposing principle of law and order as manifested in history through various leaders and governments. Where this principle of law (under which we live here in the United States and Canada) breaks down the Man of Lawlessness will give full vent to his evil, and only the return of Christ will stop and end it.

When we put these ideas together we see a historical pattern emerge:

- God's word is preached and from it many laws are formed to reflect it.
- The principle of evil is at work essentially opposing God and seen in its constant attack against moral and legal standards.
- The apostasy begins and throughout history works to a point where there is little divine basis for the laws and morals of mankind (i.e. same sex marriage, abortion, fanatical religious aggression).
- This removal of God's will from the fabric of human affairs and laws permits a final surge of evil which is personified in a single person or movement that seeks to replace God and His will as the source for human values and laws.
- This signals the return of Christ and His Word to its preeminent position and destroys once and for all:
    - The principle of evil
    - The Man of Lawlessness
    - The corrupted world
    - The wicked and unbelievers who have served the apostasy and the principle of evil

I prefer this final theory to explain Paul's prophecy because:

1. The Emperors of Rome are gone.
2. Satan cannot be divided.
3. The Papacy fails the complete description of the Man of Lawlessness.

4. It explains the past, present and future without violating any of the facts about the Man of Lawlessness and the Apostasy.

We can choose what we believe works here, but I think that the fourth theory more accurately explains most of the facts we have about this teaching.

Summary

We live in a time when both the Apostasy and the principle of evil are at work in our world and in the church. We need to do two things in response:

1. Stay close to the Word in all things.

2. Struggle against the principle of evil by preaching the Gospel to this world and living holy lives in order to call the lost into the light and safety of the church.

10.
WHAT IS THE DELUDING INFLUENCE?

So far in this epistle Paul has described the punishment awaiting non-believers and the wicked when Christ returns. He also reassures the Thessalonians that the "day" has not come because:

- The Apostasy had to occur first
- The Man of Lawlessness had to be revealed

In the previous chapter I mentioned several ideas concerning these events:

- The Apostasy (the falling away from the Christian faith) has already begun and is quite active in the world.
- The Man of Lawlessness has not yet been revealed, however the mystery of lawlessness is at work in the world creating great evil and wickedness.

I said that we will know the end is the next step (we know the sequence, not the time frame) when we see this lawless power in the world manifested in a person or entity who will be so evil and powerful that he will, in some way, claim equality with God.

This face of evil, Man of Lawlessness, will deceive nations to the point where the truth of Christ and the church will be seriously threatened. It will be at this juncture (when this lawless one will be revealed to Christians for who he really is) that Christ will return to destroy this person and bring His church with Him to eternal glory in heaven, and send the wicked, the unbelievers and those deluded by the Man of Lawlessness to hell.

Now in his description of these times Paul also mentions another idea that is hard to understand. He says that God will send a "deluding influence" on those who refuse to love the truth so that these people will be judged and condemned on account of the lie that they believed.

> For this reason God will send upon them a deluding influence so that they will believe what is false, in order that they all may be judged who did not believe the truth, but took pleasure in wickedness.
> - II Thessalonians 2:11-12

At first glance it would seem that God forces people to believe a lie and then punishes them for it. This doesn't seem fair. Is there a solution? There is, but you need to understand how God's will functions in order to make sense of this passage.

The Will of God - II Thessalonians 2:11-12

The Bible explains the unusual way that God's will operates in His relationship with mankind and the material universe. There are two sides to God's will:

1. God's Direct Will

Some things are done in concert with the operation of God's direct will. This direct will functions in two different modes:

A. God's Direct Positive Will - God wills directly for good things to happen. For example, God wills the creation into being and it is good; God wills that Christ come to save man; God wills that His Word is recorded and preserved for mankind. God directly wills these good things to happen. In these we see God's direct positive will happening.

B. God's Direct Negative Will - God wills directly for judgment and punishment to happen. For example, God directly wills the flood to come and destroy the earth; God sends the plagues to punish the Pharaoh; God uses different nations to judge and punish His people throughout the ages. God directly wills negative things to happen to accomplish His justice and His purposes. So God directly wills both positive and negative things to happen in the material universe and to mankind.

2. God's Permissive Will

Many events in the Bible and in history occur, but do so in cooperation with God's permissive will. This permissive will also operates in two different modes:

A. God's Permissive Positive Will - A church was planted in Choctaw, Oklahoma in 1939 and years later the Choctaw church supports a missionary in Montreal to help build up a church in Quebec. There was no inspiration or revelation or miracle here. This was done according to God's permissive positive will. Men are the ones who decided to do it and God's permissive positive will allowed it to happen.

My wife and I decided to have a family. We decided to have four children (not three, not five or six, just four) and God's permissive positive will allowed us this blessing. He could have stopped us, but He didn't. He allowed this good and positive thing to happen.

B. God's Permissive Negative Will - Some things God permits, but they are not things He devises or likes. He permits and uses these nevertheless to accomplish His ultimate purpose. For example, Satan tempts Eve, attacks Job, manipulates the principle of evil in the world. God did not devise and will these things, but in His sovereignty He permitted Satan to do these things. There are illnesses, accidents and tragedies that happen in the world. God does not will these things, directly invent or send them, but He does permit these negative consequences of sin to affect us in different ways.

And so, God consciously wills certain positive and negative things to happen and He also permits certain positive and negative things to happen which He does not devise but does permit to take place. However, regardless of what happens and under which direction of His will a certain thing falls, God knows in advance what He will directly do and what He will permit others to do. He also knows the consequences and outworking of all that is done and how He will use everything in order to glorify Himself and accomplish His ultimate will, which is to justify the faith of the saints in Christ and punish the wicked and disbelievers.

So when we talk about the "delusion" sent on the people by God, we have to take what I've just said into consideration in order to understand what Paul is saying here. This delusion is sent under God's permissive negative will. God is permitting the deceiver (Man of Lawlessness) to capture completely through his lies and deceptions, all of those who do not love the truth. God doesn't invent the delusion, doesn't lie, doesn't approve of the deceiver, but He allows him to function for a time in the world. Those who believe the lies will be allowed to do so without interference from God. These will be judged and judged rightly because they preferred to believe the lies rather than the truth.

The truth, willed directly by God and gloriously revealed by Christ is so superior to the lie, but these preferred to believe the lie, so God permitted them to believe it to the fullest. God "sends the delusion" in the sense that He permits it to happen at the hands of the deceiver, and He permits it to work fully on those who choose to believe it rather than the superior truth sent directly by God.

In the end, this full acceptance of the lie will prove His judgment to be obvious, just, necessary and without doubt. There will be no doubt or sorrow that these people deserve what they get at judgment.

Once Paul finishes describing the events preceding the return of Christ and the condemnation of those not ready for His return because of their disbelief, he turns his attention to the Thessalonians themselves. Since these things are, and will be in this way, he urges the Thessalonians not to become like the ones who love the lies (and what the lies permit them to do) but rather, follow the path taken by those who love the truth and go where that road will lead them.

The Way of Truth - II Thessalonians 2:13-17

> But we should always give thanks to God for you, brethren beloved by the Lord, because God has chosen you from the beginning for salvation through sanctification by the Spirit and faith in the truth. It was for this He called you through our gospel, that you may gain the glory of our Lord Jesus Christ. So then, brethren, stand firm and hold to the traditions which you were taught, whether by word of mouth or by letter from us. Now may our Lord Jesus Christ Himself and God our Father, who has loved us and given us eternal comfort and good hope by grace, comfort and strengthen your hearts in every good work and word.
> - II Thessalonians 2:13-17

Paul reviews the situation and tells them that even though there is a wickedness and danger in the world, there is still reason to be thankful – especially for the church in Thessalonica. He gives two basic reasons.

1. They have been chosen for salvation – vs. 13

Here, God's choosing is not in a judicial or arbitrary sense where one chooses someone or something over someone or something else. Paul refers to the phenomenon where God appropriates or chooses for Himself those who are being sanctified by the Holy Spirit because they trust the truth of the Gospel. God will choose/appropriate everyone who does this without prejudice. He will choose for Himself all who choose to believe in Christ and has promised to do so from before the beginning of time.

In this verse Paul also says that those who are subject to God's choice of them are those who are transformed by the Spirit because of their confidence in what is true. This is different from the attempt at transforming themselves using systems or methods that cannot accomplish the transformation required by God. For example, people who try to change themselves by using:

- The Law (legalism or perfectionism)
- Magic (manipulation of the spirits)
- Idolatry (worship of the created)
- Philosophy (man-made truths and systems for self actualization)

They can be thankful that because of their faith in the truth of the Gospel (God's solution to sin and death) they have become the chosen ones of God and heirs of salvation. This change is real, personal, eternal and spiritual.

2. Their salvation is sure – vs. 14

The salvation they have will manifest itself fully when Jesus returns. The nature of this salvation is such that when He returns they will share in His glory. This is what the present transformation (sanctification) is working towards, what Christ will complete when He returns. This was the original intention of God's calling of them through the Gospel: that one day they would be perfected in glory. This final perfection, this completion of their spiritual transformation is a sure thing, there is no doubt that it will take place so they should be thankful for this.

In verse 15, Paul summarizes by saying that if these things are true then don't be fooled by lies. This is how you are to respond to the lies that are trying to disturb your faith, lies that are deceiving others.

1. **Stand firm** – be mature, strong, unmoved. Don't lose your composure.

2. **Hold to traditions** – hang on to what they were originally taught by their teachers and mentors: Paul, Timothy and Sylvanus.

He completes the passage with a blessing:

> Now may our Lord Jesus Christ Himself and God our Father, who has loved us and given us eternal comfort and good hope by grace, comfort and strengthen your hearts in every good work and word.
> - II Thessalonians 2:16-17

He prays that the same God and Christ who have given them their love will also comfort them with the knowledge that they are saved by grace eternally. He also prays that God will exercise His (direct positive) will in encouraging them when they are discouraged, and help them in what they are to say and do.

Yes, there are lies and condemnation for some, but Paul is thankful that they are saved and he prays that God will help them stay that way, using His direct positive will. God will not just let good things happen – He will make good things happen!

Will and Salvation

This passage is unusual in that within it are listed five things that God does and three things that we do in regards to our salvation. God's direct positive will operates in five different ways in regards to our salvation:

1. He loves - vs. 13

The motivation for God saving us is love. He consciously, willfully, purposefully loves each soul.

2. He chooses - vs. 13

As we said, this means that He takes for Himself. At the beginning God chose all those who would believe the truth to be saved. He deliberately chose this group to experience the glory of heaven.

3. He calls - vs. 14

God intentionally calls everyone to glory through the Gospel. Those who love the truth respond to the Gospel.

4. He saves - vs. 13

I Timothy 2:4 says that God wants all to be saved, this is His ultimate purpose. He provides everything we need for the complete transformation and salvation of the soul.

5. He glorifies - vs. 14

His ultimate goal is that all who respond to the call will become glorious like His Son Jesus.

Now in all of these acts God's "direct will" is in operation, and the significance of this for us is that if these things are God's direct positive will, then our salvation is certain because:

- God always loves – even when we are weak
- God never changes His choice – no surprises
- God continues to call – He wants all saved
- God guarantees salvation – we can trust Him

- God has the power to transform us into glory – we have something to look forward to

On the opposite side of this relationship we see that man also has his direct will in operation when it comes to salvation. It operates in three ways:

1. **Man believes –** These Thessalonians chose to believe (accepted as true) the message of the Gospel. There is nothing we can do to save ourselves, no work or good deed can be exchanged for our souls. However, God asks of us not what we cannot do, He asks us what we can do, and exercising our positive direct will in believing and acting on that belief (repentance and baptism) is something we all can do.

2. **Man gives thanks (vs. 13) –** The giving of thanks for our blessings is part of the direct operation of our will, and an expression of faith. Not to give thanks is usually the first sign of a loss of faith (Romans 1).

3. **Man stands firm in truth –** We do not exchange something or do something to earn or maintain our salvation. We merely hold on to what has been given to us freely by God. We do this by retaining the truth of the gospel as it has been given to us by Christ, and avoiding the lies and deceptions that try to deny the Gospel and its power.

Man's direct will can reject God's love, refuse His choice, ignore His call, neglect His salvation and resist the transformation of one's soul into glory. When man directly opposes God in this way, God's passive negative will allows man to resist Him and suffer the consequences.

Summary

God's direct will was operating from the beginning with the purpose of saving the Thessalonians, and in spite of their difficulties, so long as they held firm in the truth, God would ultimately complete His direct will: their glorious resurrection and eternal life with Christ in heaven.

Lessons

1. It is God's will to save us but is it always our will to be saved?

    - Do we reject His love by loving sin?

    - Refuse His choice by choosing something other than Christ?

    - Ignore His call by putting off our decision?

    - Resist the work of the Spirit within us?

2. God is in charge of our salvation from beginning to end. Don't worry, be happy. Our job is to trust the truth (Jesus is God, the cross saves us, we will be resurrected).

3. Comfort and strength comes from God not from things. The only way things can comfort us is when we do good things and say good things, not when we acquire nice things.

The point for us in all of this is that God's direct will operates for us in the same way and power as it did with the Thessalonians. Let's not be overwhelmed by the power of evil in the world – let's have confidence that God is in charge and He will save us. Let's be careful not to believe lies but to remain faithful to what we have received from Christ and His apostles. Let's ask God to directly strengthen and comfort us in the doing of good and saying of good so we can be found busy in these things when Christ returns. If we do, we'll be ready for the second coming.

11.

THE JUDGEMENT DAY

This series has tried to present an in-depth study of the two letters that Paul wrote to the church in Thessalonica. In both letters Paul describes in detail the second coming of Christ and the events surrounding it. At this point I would like to add to the information that Paul provides in these epistles by reviewing a passage from the gospel of Matthew that addresses this same topic: the Second Coming and the Judgment. Jesus speaks about His return and the end of the world in Matthew 24-25.

> Jesus came out from the temple and was going away when His disciples came up to point out the temple buildings to Him. And He said to them, "Do you not see all these things? Truly I say to you, not one stone here will be left upon another, which will not be torn down." As he was sitting on the Mount of Olives, the disciples came to Him privately, saying, "Tell us, when will these things happen, and what will be the sign of Your coming, and of the end of the age?
> - Matthew 24:1-3

In this passage Matthew describes a scene where Jesus is leaving the temple area and as He leaves the Apostles point out the magnificent buildings of the temple, which He has just said will one day be deserted. During that period the temple had undergone extensive reconstruction work; the latest effort being paid for by Herod himself.

In verse 1 Jesus responds to their comments by saying that the buildings will not only be empty, they will be torn down. This sets up further questions by the Apostles (Peter, James, John and Andrew - Matthew 13:13) who wanted more information about what He had just told them. In their dialogue the Apostles questioned Him about two things:

1. When will the temple be destroyed?
2. What signs will accompany the end of the world that will be brought on by the Second Coming?

Now, whether the Apostles thought these two events would happen at the same time or at different times, we do not know. We do know from their questions that they were asking about two different events:

- The destruction of the temple.
- The return of the Lord at the end of the world.

The following section in Matthew can be confusing so it helps if we divide it into the three views of history that Jesus spoke of in answering their questions.

1. Panoramic View – vs. 4-14

> And Jesus answered and said to them, "See to it that no one misleads you. For many will come in My name, saying, 'I am the Christ,' and will mislead many. You will be hearing of wars and rumors of wars. See that you are not frightened, for those things must take place, but that is not yet the end. For nation will rise against nation, and kingdom against kingdom, and in various places there will be famines and earthquakes. But all these things are merely the beginning of birth pangs. Then they will deliver you to tribulation, and will kill you, and you will be hated by all nations because of My name. At that time many will fall away and will betray one another and hate one another. Many false prophets will arise and will mislead many. Because lawlessness is increased, most people's love will grow cold. But the one who endures to the end, he will be saved. This gospel of the kingdom shall be preached in the whole world as a testimony to all the nations,

> and then the end will come.
> - Matthew 24:4-14

In these verses Jesus describes an overview or panoramic view of world history that includes the time before the destruction of the temple, the time after the destruction and the period at the end of time when He will return.

2. Telescope to Jerusalem View – vs. 15-35

> Therefore when you see the ABOMINATION OF DESOLATION which was spoken of through Daniel the prophet, standing in the holy place (let the reader understand), then those who are in Judea must flee to the mountains. Whoever is on the housetop must not go down to get the things out that are in his house. Whoever is in the field must not turn back to get his cloak. But woe to those who are pregnant and to those who are nursing babies in those days! But pray that your flight will not be in the winter, or on a Sabbath. For then there will be a great tribulation, such as has not occurred since the beginning of the world until now, nor ever will. Unless those days had been cut short, no life would have been saved; but for the sake of the elect those days will be cut short. Then if anyone says to you, "Behold, here is the Christ, or There He is,' do not believe him. For false Christs and false prophets will arise and will show great signs and wonders, so as to mislead, if possible, even the elect. Behold, I have told you in advance. So if they say to you, 'Behold, He is in the wilderness,' do not go out, or, 'Behold, He is in the inner rooms,' do not believe them. For just as the lightning comes from the east and flashes even to the west, so will the coming of the Son of Man be. Wherever the corpse is, there the vultures will gather.

> But immediately after the tribulation of those days THE SUN WILL BE DARKENED, AND THE MOON WILL NOT GIVE ITS LIGHT, AND THE STARS WILL FALL from the sky, and the powers of the heavens will be shaken. And then the sign of the Son of Man will appear in the sky, and then all the tribes of the earth will mourn, and they will see THE SON OF MAN COMING ON THE CLOUDS OF THE SKY with power and great glory. And He will send forth His angels with A GREAT TRUMPET and THEY WILL GATHER TOGETHER His elect from the four winds, from one end of the sky to the other.
>
> Now learn the parable from the fig tree: when its branch has already become tender and puts forth its leaves, you know that summer is near; so, you too, when you see all these things, recognize that He is near, right at the door. Truly I say to you, this generation will not pass away until all these things take place. Heaven and earth will pass away, but My words will not pass away.
> - Matthew 24:15-35

In these verses Jesus telescopes or focuses on one great event in the history of the Jews: the destruction of Jerusalem, which we know took place in 70 AD, some 40 years into the future.

3. Telescope to the Second Coming – vs. 36-44

> But of that day and hour no one knows, not even the angels of heaven, nor the Son, but the Father alone. For the coming of the Son of Man will be just like the days of Noah. For as in those days before the flood they were eating and drinking, marrying and giving in marriage, until the day that Noah entered the ark, and they did not understand until the flood came and took them all away; so will the coming of the Son of Man

> be. Then there will be two men in the field; one will be taken and one will be left. Two women will be grinding at the mill; one will be taken and one will be left.
>
> Therefore be on the alert, for you do not know which day your Lord is coming. But be sure of this, that if the head of the house had known at what time of the night the thief was coming, he would have been on the alert and would not have allowed his house to be broken into. For this reason you also must be ready; for the Son of Man is coming at an hour when you do not think He will.
> - Matthew 24:36-44

Jesus finishes with a look to the far future when He will return ushering in the end of days and the judgment. If we keep these three views in mind it will help us to untangle these complex verses.

Panorama Until Second Coming – vs. 4-15

Vs. 4 – This instruction is given so that they will know and avoid false teachers and prophets in these matters.

Vs. 5-8 – The cycle of false prophets, wars and troubles in the world will continue until the end but these in themselves are not the signs – they are only the beginning of things that will get progressively worse before not only the end of Jerusalem comes, but also the end of the world comes.

Vs. 9-12 – Parallel to II Thessalonians where Paul talks about the end of the world and what must take place first:

- Apostasy (falling away, love grows cold)
- Man of Lawlessness who deceives many through false signs and tries to take the place of God – he will be revealed.

- Jesus describes the devolution of the world (a cycle of evil and revival that continue to play out in human history until during a period of extreme evil the cycle is broken by the appearance of Jesus signaling the end of the world, it's destruction, the resurrection and judgement of all mankind with condemnation for some and glory for disciples)

Vs. 13 – In contrast, He promises that the faithful will be saved despite these trials and evil.

Vs. 14 – He also promises that the great commission will be carried out and must be carried out before the end can/will come.

This is a panoramic view of the events and flow of history that will occur until His second coming.

Telescope to Fall of Jerusalem – vs. 15-35

Judea was rebellious and longed to return to the glory days of independence and power experienced by the nation during the time of Solomon's reign. This caused such unrest that Rome sent in troops to quell the rebellion. From 66-70 AD the Roman armies successfully laid siege to Jerusalem and totally destroyed the city and temple along with over 1 million people. This destruction of the Jewish nation and its principle city and temple was the fulfillment of Jesus' prophecy to the disciples years earlier, described in this passage. The disciples wanted to know when this would happen and Jesus gives them the "signs" to watch out for, because many of them would still be alive when it would happen.

Vs. 1-18 – The first sign was the Abomination of Desolation. The point was that when the temple would be desecrated this would be a sign that destruction was near and they should escape the city. The prophet Daniel (Daniel 11:31; 12:11) had prophesied that the temple would be defiled and it was in the days of the Maccabees by the Syrian king, Antiochus

Epiphanes, who sacrificed a pig on the altar of the temple. Jesus picks up this idea and says that in the same way when the temple will be defiled by Gentiles during their lifetimes, it will be the signal to escape.

> But when you see Jerusalem surrounded by armies,
> then recognize that her desolation is near.
> - Luke 21:20

Luke 21:20 tells us that the surrounding of the temple by foreign armies is what constituted defilement. The standards or shields of the Roman army were idolatrous and often used for worship by the soldiers. Surrounding the temple with these would desecrate it. Many scholars differ here as to what the "abomination" was, and refer to Jewish historians for events that occurred before, during or after the siege that could fit, but Luke 21:20 is the only biblical reference that is suitable in this context.

"He who reads" means he who reads Daniel and, along with Christ's cryptogram, will be able to know when it is time to escape. In 68 AD the majority of Christians living in Jerusalem escaped to Pella, a city located in modern day Jordan, and thus avoid being killed in the massacre.

Vs. 19-21 – The tribulation refers to the suffering caused by the Roman siege of the city.

- Over 1 million killed

- The combination of the gravity of their sin (Jews who received the blessings and promises but rejected and killed their Messiah) along with the horror of the punishment (nation wiped out) has not been equaled.

Vs. 22 – God's providence permitted this war to end so that the Christians would not also be annihilated along with the Jews. In their attack, the Roman soldiers made no distinction between Christian and non-Christian Jews.

Vs. 23-26 – The believers would naturally associate the destruction of Jerusalem with the return of Jesus, so the Lord warns them against being deceived by those who would claim to be the Lord or speak from God. Josephus, a Jewish historian of the time, writes about this period where rumors of the Messiah coming or being present circulated in order to keep the people in the city. The Roman threat created hysteria and fear that in turn produced many "prophets" who claimed visions and messages from God. One such prophet said that he would miraculously separate the Sea of Galilee and 25,000 people followed him out.

Vs. 27 – Jesus tells them that when He does return (not in 70 AD but at the end of the world) it will be evident to all, like lightning across the sky. Everyone will easily and readily know that it is He.

Vs. 28 – The corpse is the Jewish nation, the vultures are the false Christs and prophets. When you see them in abundance, this will be a second sign that the end of Jerusalem is near.

Vs. 29 – The first word in this verse presents a problem to some: Immediately. If we make this next section a discussion about the end of the world and the second coming of Jesus, then it must occur right after the destruction of Jerusalem (some believe and teach Jesus had already returned). Since the Man of Lawlessness has not been revealed, Jesus has not returned, therefore this passage must still be talking about events surrounding the destruction of Jerusalem not the end of the world.

Vs. 30-31 – Therefore verses 29-31 speak about the destruction and the effects that it will have on both believers and non-believers. The language is Apocalyptic and is used by prophets to describe cataclysmic historical and political events (Isaiah 13 describes the destruction of Babylon in similar language). Language using the symbolism of the destruction of heavenly bodies is used to describe the very real fate of the world at the end (II Peter 3:10), but also the end and destruction of nations on the earth. In this case the end of the Jewish nation as a people under God's special care.

The coming of the Son of Man refers to both the second coming at the end of the world as well as any judgment that God makes on a particular nation throughout history; in this case the nation of Israel in 70 AD. It also fits the context of this passage. The Jews who rejected Him now will see him coming as a form of judgment on their nation, a terrible catastrophe that would horrify the world but liberate Christians and the Gospel from Jewish persecution.

Note that the Greek word translated "angel" can also be translated as "messenger." This verse can be seen as prophecy concerning the spreading of the Gospel throughout the world after the fall of Jerusalem. Verse 14 said this needed to be done before Christ returned and now with the ideological and cultural restraints of Judaism removed, Christianity would flourish even more.

Vs. 32-35 – Jesus warns them to pay attention to the signs that He has given them because these things will happen in their generation, and He promises by His word that they will happen!

Telescope to Second Coming – vs. 36-44

Jesus has just explained the signs that will preview the destruction of Jerusalem:

1. Preaching of Gospel to all nations (Romans 10:18)

2. Multiplication of false Christs (historian Josephus)

3. Abomination of Temple (Luke 2:20)

4. Great tribulation (historian Josephus)

In verses 36-44 He makes a contrast of this event with the second coming at the end of the world.

Vs. 36 – No one knows the time, not even Jesus while He is with His disciples. This refers to His second coming, not the destruction of Jerusalem in 70 AD.

Vs. 37-39 – There will be no cataclysmic signs and all will seem normal. Normal in the sense that the believers will be preparing themselves for the second coming and the end of the world, and the rest of the world will be ignoring it until it will be too late (just like in the time of Noah).

Vs. 40-41 – Some take this verse to mean that before Jesus returns some will be taken in a "Rapture" and disappear to be with God in heaven. This is part of the Pre-millenialist view of the rapture and 1,000 year reign. In context, however, Jesus is talking about readiness and He says that when He returns suddenly, one will be saved and one lost – no time for repentance and change. Just like Noah, when the rain came they were taken and disappeared into the ark, the others remained to die in the flood. When Jesus comes, the faithful will be taken to be with Him and the disbelievers immediately put away from His presence.

Vs. 42-44 – Since the end is to be like this we should always be prepared and not foolishly lapse into sin thinking we have plenty of time to repent. Christians need to be ready for His return because no one knows when it will be.

Exhortations to Vigilance – Matthew 24:45-25:30

After responding to the question of the judgment on Jerusalem and His return, Jesus warns them to be vigilant and does so with three parables:

1. **Parable of the evil slave (vs. 45-51) -** Here the lesson is not to presume we have the luxury of sinning because the end is far away, it can come at any time and the judgment is sure for those who are unfaithful.

2. **Parable of the 10 virgins (25:1-13) -** Here Jesus warns against the foolishness of not being ready. In this parable it is not a question of gross evil, but rather of negligence. To neglect Christ will bring destruction in the end as well.

3. **Parable of the talents (vs. 14-30) -** Here the warning is for those who are in the Kingdom of God (church), but who fail to expand its borders and fail to serve the king with zeal. This slave was not caught or surprised unprepared, he just assumed that his preparation was sufficient when it wasn't.

All three parables have the element of preparation, judgment and punishment for those who neglect to prepare for the return of the Master.

Judgment Scene – 25:31-46

The climax of the discourse is the judgment scene at the end of the world. Those found to be righteous have obeyed the commands to love God (refer to Him as Lord) as well as their neighbor. This was the way to prepare. Those condemned have the same judgment and are condemned because they did not love their neighbor.

The punishment and reward is eternal in nature. The overarching theme is: Be Ready.

12.
BE READY

So far in these two letters Paul has:

1. Given thanks for their faithfulness in spite of persecution and trials.

2. Defended his own conduct against false accusations.

3. Instructed them concerning the return of Jesus.

    - Before Jesus returns – the Apostasy – Man of Lawlessness revealed

    - When Jesus returns – believers caught up – wicked punished

4. He has also encouraged them to remain steadfast, in the meantime: continue believing the truth and follow the path of truth in order to avoid the destruction awaiting those who follow the path of lies and deception.

After these instructions Paul leaves them with two final exhortations as he closes his epistle.

Exhortation #1 – Pray

> 1 Finally, brethren, pray for us that the word of the Lord
> will spread rapidly and be glorified, just as it did also
> with you; 2 and that we will be rescued from perverse
> and evil men; for not all have faith. 3 But the Lord is
> faithful, and He will strengthen and protect you from
> the evil one. 4 We have confidence in the Lord
> concerning you that you are doing and will continue to

> do what we command. [5] May the Lord direct your heart into the love of God and into the steadfastness of Christ.
> - II Thessalonians 3:1-5

Paul has begun this letter by praying for them, now he closes the letter by asking them to pray for him. He guides them in the things to pray for:

Vs. 1 – That the Gospel will grow and spread as it did with them (church growth begins with prayer, then and now).

Vs. 2 – That Paul will be delivered from those who oppose the gospel because of lack of faith (the world opposes the church, then and now).

Vs. 3 – He reassures them concerning the things he has spoken (be assured that it will all happen, don't doubt).

Paul knew that the Gospel is God's powerful tool to save man, but prayer is what keeps the Gospel in motion and being spread. You can't save people just by praying for them; somewhere along the way you have to preach the Gospel to them. They have to know the terms of their salvation. They have to be confronted with the painful truth that unless they obey the Gospel and follow Christ they are lost. We have to risk telling them this, and take the chance that they will be upset with us or reject and even humiliate us.

There is no salvation without the Gospel, but there is no Gospel being sent without prayer. Jesus prayed that God would send workers (Matthew 9:37-38).

Vs. 4-5 – In the last verses of this section Paul reminds them that God will answer their prayers. And in answer to their prayers God will not only guard Paul, but will also guard them and help them to grow in love and perseverance. These then, are the type of things we should also be praying for ourselves.

Exhortation #2 – Stay Busy in Doing Good

Vs. 6 – Paul describes the problem they are having and how to handle it. They should remain aloof (means to mark off a boundary) from those who are living disorderly lives (not according to what they had been taught). What had they been taught?

- Faithfulness, good works
- Prayer, purity
- Not to unnecessarily be a burden to others

We must remember that in the first letter Paul had admonished those who were not working to get busy and quietly support themselves (I Thessalonians 4:11). Apparently some still believed that the end was at hand and did not obey this admonition. Paul, in the name of Christ, commands the church to take action. In this section he describes five things they should be busy doing:

1. Remain aloof (stay away)

> Now we command you, brethren, in the name of our Lord Jesus Christ, that you keep away from every brother who leads an unruly life and not according to the tradition which you received from us.
> - II Thessalonians 3:6

We've already mentioned this one. They are to note and withdraw from lazy, undisciplined, unrepentant Christians so that their behavior is made public and dealt with. This is not easy to do but very effective when done in a proper and loving way.

2. Follow the example of the Apostles

> For you yourselves know how you ought to follow our example, because we did not act in an undisciplined manner among you, nor did we eat anyone's bread without paying for it, but with labor and hardship we kept working night and day so that we would not be a burden to any of you; not because we do not have the right to this, but in order to offer ourselves as a model for you, so that you would follow our example.
> - II Thessalonians 3:7-9

The Apostles are the living examples that Christ left for us to follow. We copy Christ when we copy the examples of their lives and their faith.

3. Remember and obey the teaching

> For even when we were with you, we used to give you this order: if anyone is not willing to work, then he is not to eat, either. For we hear that some among you are leading an undisciplined life, doing no work at all, but acting like busybodies. Now such persons we command and exhort in the Lord Jesus Christ to work in quiet fashion and eat their own bread.
> - II Thessalonians 3:10-12

The Apostles taught on the subject of right living in the Lord; remember this teaching and teach it to the ones who need to obey it…on all matters.

4. Don't be discouraged

> But as for, brethren, do not grow weary of doing good.
> - II Thessalonians 3:13

Don't be tired of doing good, working hard and encouraging those who are not doing good and working hard. God will reward you – this is His promise, so don't quit.

5. Discipline those who refuse to repent

> If anyone does not obey our instruction in this letter, take special note of that person and do not associate with him, so that he will be put to shame. Yet do not regard him as an enemy, but admonish him as a brother.
> - II Thessalonians 3:14-15

They had to continue to warn and teach the disobedient and unrepentant one while remaining separated from him. They had to do this unpleasant task and still remember that he was a brother and needed to be disciplined in love. One of the reasons that there is often division and trouble in the church is the reluctance to discipline correctly those members who are not following the teachings of Christ. These became like a cancer on the body, robbing it of strength and health.

Obviously, this is a short list of the type of things Christians ought to be doing, but the Thessalonian Christians definitely had to focus on these areas in order to remain viable as a church.

Closing Remarks

Paul has thanked, taught, exhorted, and now he closes his letter with a variety of thoughts that the Thessalonians needed to ponder.

> Now may the Lord of peace Himself continually grant you peace in every circumstance. The Lord be with you all!
> - II Thessalonians 3:16

God is with them in every situation. His presence is what brings them the peace they feel and want to remain in.

> I, Paul, write this greeting with my own hand, and this is a distinguishing mark in every letter; this is the way I write.
> - II Thessalonians 3:17

This letter is genuine. They may have received fake reports in the past which led to confusion and disturbed their sense of peace, but his letter is true. They can therefore follow its instructions with confidence. He probably had someone else write the letter as he dictated and then signed it with his own hand (2:2). Some think that his "thorn" in the flesh was poor eyesight that necessitated this and produced the unusual signature he talks about.

> The grace of our Lord Jesus Christ be with you all.
> - II Thessalonians 3:18

He offers a final blessing on the church. If they have the Lord's favor upon them, there is nothing that can harm them, and their blessings and future are secure.

Summary

In this final chapter Paul describes a people who have believed the truth and this truth is what separates them from those who are in darkness and who will be punished when Jesus returns. In this closing portion Paul does three things:

1. He encourages them to pray that the truth will continue to spread. Prayer is the fuel of the Gospel and Paul wants them to pray to this end.

2. He commands them to take action against those who are living in a disorderly way within the church.

3. He exhorts them to follow his example in the way they live their everyday lives.

The theme for these lessons in I and II Thessalonians has been "Be Ready" because the Lord is coming. Note that Paul, in the closing section of his second letter actually spells out the type of things all Christians need to be doing in order to – Be Ready:

1. Believe the Truth

The reason people perish is because they ultimately end up believing a lie. For example, they believe as true that:

- Jesus in not God
- Jesus in not Lord
- Jesus in not Savior
- God will not punish sinners
- There is no god

It is the belief of what is false that condemns a person in the end. In order to believe the truth however, we need to:

- Want to believe the truth – Hebrews 11:6
- We must hear it – John 17:17; Romans10:17
- We must obey it – Matthew 7:21

In order to continue believing what is true we need to:

- Continue hearing God's word – I Peter 2:2
- Continue obeying God's word – John 15:6-7

Believing the truth is not a once in a lifetime event like baptism. It is an on-going process. In this process we grow deeper in appreciation and understanding of God's word as we continue in study and obedience. You cannot appropriate truth without corresponding obedience. Growth in the knowledge of God's truth requires obedience to God's truth.

As you believe, so you become. What you believe changes you only when you respond to it in obedience. In order to be ready we must also…

2. Pray Always

Paul prayed for them, they prayed for him. As Christians we must be strong in prayer if we are to be truly ready. We have more good reasons to constantly pray than the one reference in Thessalonians. We pray because:

- Jesus, God's Son, prayed often – Matthew 26:36
- Satan is powerful and always at work – I Peter 5:8
- God commands us to do it – I Thessalonians 5:17
- God answers prayer. It works! – James 5:16

In the letter to the Ephesians, Paul tells us that the battles we as Christians fight are not physical – even if the battlefield is the physical world. The wars and conflicts here on earth are the results of spiritual activities going on in the spiritual realm (Ephesians 6:12). The armies of the earth fight many battles here but are of no consequence in affecting the spiritual warfare above.

It is the Lord's army who does battle with these heavenly forces through prayer, that has a direct effect on the spiritual warfare taking place here on earth.

Be ready by believing the truth, by on-going prayer and by…

3. Staying Busy

We give ourselves lots of excuses not to work hard, not to make an effort, always taking the easy way out. If we realized that laziness is a major contributor to the three D's that are a curse on our society and in our families: depression, discouragement and division.

Whether it be in society, in our families, or in the church – laziness contributes to the three D's that end up destroying these institutions. Many times it isn't the actual work that's missing but the willingness to work that's missing. In every parable on the subject of the sudden return of Christ, one of the key ideas is that the acceptable or ready servants who received a blessing from the Master upon his sudden return was the one who was busy.

There is a question that both epistles to the Thessalonians ask us, "**Are You Ready?**" Are you ready for Christ's return in the sense that you are busy:

- In the study, knowledge and obedience to your faith.
- In your devotion to prayer. John was praying when the Lord appeared to him in a heavenly scene.
- In your hard work on behalf of the Gospel and the Church.

Let us remember that Jesus will return and when He does these are the things He will be looking for among those who claim to be His disciples.

The lessons are now yours and I pray that you will all be ready for Him when He comes.

BibleTalk.tv is an Internet Mission Work.

We provide textual Bible teaching material on our website and mobile apps for free. We enable churches and individuals all over the world to have access to high quality Bible materials for personal growth, group study or for teaching in their classes.

The goal of this mission work is to spread the gospel to the greatest number of people using the latest technology available. For the first time in history it is becoming possible to preach the gospel to the entire world at once. BibleTalk.tv is an effort to preach the gospel to all nations every day until Jesus returns.

The Choctaw Church of Christ in Oklahoma City is the sponsoring congregation for this work and provides the recording facilities and oversight. If you wish to support this work please contact us at the address below.

bibletalk.tv/support

Made in the USA
Middletown, DE
20 August 2021

46493068R00071